D0454758

YOUNG WOMEN OF
ACHIEVEMENT

YOUNG WOMEN OF
ACHIEVEMENT

A Resource for
Girls in Science, Math,
and Technology

FRANCES A. KARNES

and

KRISTEN R. STEPHENS

 **Prometheus Books**

59 John Glenn Drive
Amherst, New York 14228-2197

Published 2002 by Prometheus Books

Young Women of Achievement: A Resource for Girls in Science, Math, and Technology. Copyright © 2002 by Frances A. Karnes and Kristen R. Stephens. All rights reserved. No part of this publication may be reproduced, stored in a retrieval system, or transmitted in any form or by any means, digital, electronic, mechanical, photocopying, recording, or otherwise, or conveyed via the Internet or a Web site without prior written permission of the publisher, except in the case of brief quotations embodied in critical articles and reviews.

Inquiries should be addressed to
Prometheus Books
59 John Glenn Drive
Amherst, New York 14228–2197
VOICE: 716–691–0133, ext. 207
FAX: 716–564–2711
WWW.PROMETHEUSBOOKS.COM

06 05 04 03 02   5 4 3 2 1

Library of Congress Cataloging-in-Publication Data

Karnes, Frances A.
    Young women of achievement : a resource for girls in science, math, and technology / Frances E. Karnes and Kristen R. Stephens.
        p. cm.
    Includes bibliographical references and index.
    ISBN 1–57392–965–4 (pbk. : alk. paper)
    1. Science—Vocational guidance. 2. Women in science. 3. Women in technology. I. Stephens, Kristen R. II. Title.

Q130 .K37 2002
500'.82—dc21

                                                                            2002020569

Printed in the United States of America on acid-free paper

TABLE OF CONTENTS

PART II—STORIES OF ACCOMPLISHMENT 29

PART III—ADDITIONAL INSPIRATION   161

PART IV—RESOURCE SECTION

ACKNOWLEDGMENTS

There are many persons who have made major contributions to the production of this publication. Our deepest appreciation is given to the girls and young women who serve as outstanding role models for others pursuing science, mathematics, and technology and who have contributed their stories. Also noteworthy are the females who offered quotations to inspire those wanting to fulfill their aspirations.

In order to find girls and young women to contribute their stories, announcements were distributed nationwide through many sources such as state associations, consultants, and girls' organizations. To all those who assisted in our search, please know of our gratitude for your efforts and successes.

Several persons were involved in the technical production of the manuscript. The University of Southern Mississippi's Frances A. Karnes Center for Gifted Studies and Sundee Goodwin and Angela Sheely at the University of North Carolina at Charlotte receive a special thank you, as well as the supportive staff at the Duke University Talent Identification Program. The faculty, staff, and students at our respective universities continue their support and encouragement for which we are grateful. We are especially thankful to our publisher without whom this book would not have been a reality.

Our families deserve a special acknowledgment for their love and inspiration throughout the process of writing this volume. Ray, John, Leighanne, Mary Ryan, Emma Leighanne, and John Morris Karnes; Rich and Jack Kozak; Alan Stephens; and Dorothy Stephens have given us hope and encouragement. The special guidance of Christopher J. Karnes and Karen and David Stephens will always be with us throughout our lives.

This book is dedicated to Mary Ryan and Emma Leighanne Karnes, and to all the girls and young women who wish to and have achieved in science, mathematics, and technology.

INTRODUCTION

The Status of Girls and Women in Science, Mathematics, and Technology

It has been predicted that by the year 2010 the need for qualified personnel in careers associated with science, mathematics, and technology will increase dramatically.[1] Women make up 45 percent of the total labor force but only 16 percent of the science and engineering labor force.[2] In order to fill future workforce demands, more women need to be recruited and retained in these fields. Efforts to encourage women to pursue careers within the realms of science, mathematics, and technology should begin early, preferably at the elementary school level. Research indicates that in elementary school, girls begin showing a lack of interest in careers in science, mathematics, and technology and are less confident in their abilities in these areas than boys despite similar levels of achievement in these areas.[3] Although girls continue to have higher grade point averages than their male counterparts, their ACT scores in mathematics and science remain below those of boys.[4] In addition, girls continue to blame their lack of achievement in these areas on their own ability (e.g., not smart enough) whereas boys site external sources (e.g., did not study) for their failure.[5] In the last year of high school, boys are more than three times more likely than girls to pursue a career in mathematics, science, or technology.[6]

ROLE MODELS IN SCIENCE, MATHEMATICS, AND TECHNOLOGY

Female role models in science, mathematics, and technology can impact a girl's decision to pursue a career in these areas.[7] Below are the names of many extraordinary women who have made significant contributions to their fields. In browsing through these names, a few should be familiar for they often appear in textbooks; however, the majority of women presented are largely unknown because of their absence from many texts but have made extremely significant accomplishments in the fields of mathematics, science, and technology. For example, in the area of science:

- *Shi Dun*, of ancient China, developed the first paper from the bark of mulberry trees;
- *Hildegard von Bingen* correctly theorized the concept of universal gravitation centuries before Isaac Newton;
- *Mary Anning* was the first female paleontologist;
- *Hertha Ayrton* was one of the first female electrical engineers who improved the working of the electric arc used in lighting of her time;
- *Lilian Moller Gilbreth* was a pioneer in the field of time-and-motion studies;
- *Barbara McClintock* developed the theory of transposition within chromosomes;
- *Myra Adele Logan* was the first woman in the world to perform open-heart surgery;
- *Gertrude Belle Elion* received forty-five patents on medicines for leukemia, herpes, malaria, gout, AIDS, and antirejection drugs for organ transplants; and,
- *Rosalind Elsie Franklin* was responsible for much of the research that led to the understanding of the structure of DNA.

In the area of mathematics:

- *Karen Uhlenbeck* was one of the few mathematicians acknowledged as an expert in theoretical physics;
- *Ruth Gentry* was the first mathematics faculty member at Vassar College to hold a Ph.D.;
- *Sophie Germain* who is best known for her work in number theory; and,
- *Elena Lucrezia Cornaro Piscopia* who is still widely quoted by other scholars and writers for her work in mathematics.

In technology:

- *Ada Byron Lovelace* is acknowledged as the first computer programmer, and the first computer language was named after her;
- *Ida Rhodes* was a pioneer in the development of the modern electronic digital computer and its use for numerical calculations;
- *Evelyn Boyd Granville* was one of the first African American women to earn a Ph.D. in mathematics from Yale University, and she developed computer programs that were used for trajectory analysis in the Mercury and Apollo Projects;
- *Annie Easley* developed and implemented computer code used in determining solar, wind, and energy projects for NASA; and,
- *Fran Allen* was a pioneer in compiler optimization.

Only in recent years has a substantial effort been given to profiling more women and minorities of accomplishment in school texts. Prior to the 1970s, most prominent individuals profiled in primary and secondary school textbooks were male and white.[8] Clearly, the need to further expose girls to such role models is essential in inspiring them to fulfill their goals in these essential areas.

Hypathia	Gertrude Elion
Mary Anning	Rosalind Franklin
Maria Mitchell	Rosalyn Sussman Yalow
Elizabeth Blackwell	Jewel Plummer Cobb
Sarah Mather	Dian Fossey
Ida Henrietta Hyde	Jane Goodall

Nettie Stevens	Valentina Tereshkova
Marie Curie	Shannon Lucid
Florence Sabin	Antonio Novello
Alice Evans	Sally Ride
Ruth Benedict	Ada Byron Lovelace
Gerty Cori	Charlotte Agnas Scott
Margaret Mead	Charlotte Barnum
Jacqueline Cochran	Winifred E. Merrill
Maria Mayer	Gertrude Mary Cox
Myra Logan	Mina Rees
Dorothy Hodgkin	Grace Hopper

Additional information on these and other women can be found in the timelines located in Part III of this book

WHY IS THIS BOOK IMPORTANT?

While recent efforts have focused on *recruiting* girls and young women into these fields, little focus has been devoted to *retaining* girls and young women once they enter degree programs and careers in these areas. Role models or mentors have proven in many instances to be a valuable component for supporting and encouraging women in their scientific, mathematic, and technological pursuits.[9] It is believed that by providing same-age peer role models and mentors for girls interested in these fields, the future retention of women in these same areas will be further enhanced. While girls have a growing number of successful role models in these fields to emulate, few have same-age peers with similar interests and aspirations with whom to share everyday experiences, ideas, and struggles faced in the sciences, mathematics, and technology. By providing girls with inspiring stories of others who faced and overcame similar challenges, the isolation and lack of support they experience may be diminished. In addition, by providing examples of extraordinary girls, we hope to create a common network in which they may share and communicate their experiences with science, mathematics, and technology endeavors.

The inspiring stories within this book were selected based on the following criteria:

- Relevance as a role model to other girls and young women;
- Representation of geographical diversity, both nationally and internationally;
- Range of examples from elementary, secondary, and postsecondary levels;
- Inclusion of a variety of fields representing mathematics, science, and technology; and,
- Selection based on the significance of their accomplishments.

HOW TO USE THIS BOOK

This book is divided into four parts. Each section provides useful tips and strategies for the reader to assist in expanding their knowledge, motivating them toward their goals, and supporting their endeavors, in science, mathematics, and technology fields.

Part I-Planning for Your Future introduces the reader to career possibilities. Discussions are offered about how careers in science, mathematics, and technology are changing due to increased specialization, overlap among subject areas, and the expanded use of technology. In addition, specific strategies in planning for a future career in these areas are provided, such as what classes to take, helpful books to read, organizations and clubs to consider joining, and suggested tips for finding a mentor.

Part II- Stories of Accomplishment includes the true personal stories and successes of girls and young women who have already distinguished themselves in science, mathematics, and technology. These inspiring stories share the struggles and achievements experienced by individuals throughout the world.

Part III- Additional Inspiration provides the reader with information for further investigation and reflection. Included within this useful section are timelines of extraordinary women; inspiring quotations from women in these fields; and sample journaling activities.

Part IV- Resource Section presents numerous other resources for further exploration relating to science, mathematics, and technology. Suggestions of books to read, Web sites to visit, organizations to join, and programs in which to participate are all included.

WORKS CITED

1. National Science Foundation. *Women, minorities, and persons with disabilities in science and engineering (NSF No. 94-333HL)*. Washington, DC: Author, 1994.

2. White, P.E. *Women and minorities in science and engineering: An update*. Washington, DC: National Science Foundation, 1992.

3. National Science Foundation. *Women, minorities, and persons with disabilities in science and engineering*.

4. American College Testing Program. *State and national trend data for students who take the ACT assessment*. Iowa City: American College Testing, 1989.

5. Larson, J. D. "I'm just not interested: Gender related responses in a high school chemistry curriculum" (paper presented at the annual meeting of the National Association for Research in Science Teaching, St. Louis, MO., April, 1999).

6. National Science Foundation. *Women, minorities, and persons with disabilties in science and engineering*.

7. Handel, R.D. "Scientist mothers and their daughters: An inquiry into one aspect of socialization and science" (paper presented at the annual meeting of the American Educational Research Association, Chicago, IL, April, 1999).

Smith, W. S. & Erb, T. O. "Effects of women science career role models on early adolescents' attitudes toward scientists and women in science," *Journal of Research in Science Teaching* 23, no. 8 (1986): 667.

8. Weitzman, L, & Rizzo, D. *Biased textbooks: A research perspective*. Washington, DC: The Research Center on Sex Roles in Education, 1974.

9. Larson, "I'm just not interested."

Part I

PLANNING FOR YOUR FUTURE

Careers in Science, Mathematics, and Technology

M any new careers in science, mathematics, and technology are created each year. The National Academy of Sciences (1996) reports that careers in these areas are characterized by constant change, and individuals entering such careers must possess the skills to adapt to these changes. Furthermore, it is recommended that individuals working in these fields stay abreast of new knowledge, current events, and future opportunities within the field. It should be recognized that fields that have a high demand for employees today, may not tomorrow.

There are numerous areas within each field in which to focus. A sampling of careers related to each of the three fields is listed on the next page. This should not be considered a comprehensive listing. Can you think of other areas to add?

Actuary
Aerospace Engineer
Agricultural Engineer
Agronomist
Anthropologist
Applied Mathematician
Archaeologist
Astronaut
Astronomer
Astrophysicist
Bacteriologist
Biochemist
Bioethicist
Biologist
Biomedical Engineer
Biometrist
Biotechnician
Botanist
Cell Biologist
Chemical Engineer
Chemist
Cinematographer
Computer Architect
Computer Programmer
Computer Scientist
Computer Theorist
Conservationist
Cryptanalyst
Data Processor
Dietician
Dentist
Earth Scientist
Ecologist
Economist
Electrical Engineer
Embryologist
Endocrinologist

Engineer
Entomologist
Environmental Scientist
Epidemiologist
Ethnologist
Financial Advisor
Forensic Entomologist
Forensic Scientist
Forester
Geneticist
Geologist
Geophysicist
Geoscientist
Herpetologist
Horticulturalist
Ichthyologist
Immunologist
Limnologist
Mammologist
Marine Biologist
Mechanical Engineer
Medical Technician
Meteorologist
Microbiologist
Molecular Biologist
Morphologist
Mycologist
Naturalist
Nuclear Physicist
Nurse
Oceanographer
Operations Research Analyst
Ornithologist
Paleontologist
Parasitologist
Pathologist
Pharmacist

Psychologist

Physician

Physicist

Physiologist

Professor of science, mathematics, or technology fields

Research Scientist

Software Engineer

Statistician

Systems Analyst

Systems Engineer

Theoretical Mathematician

Veterinarian

Virologist

Web Page Designer

Zoologist

Some of these areas are more familiar than others. Many of these areas have resulted from a combination of two separate fields: biotechnology (biology + technology) is the use of microorganisms, such as bacteria, to perform specific industrial or manufacturing processes like the use of genetically altered bacteria to clean up spills; biochemistry (biology + chemistry) is the study of chemical substances occurring in living organisms; forensic science (biology + law enforcement) is the use of science or technology in a court of law to solve a crime; and biometry (biology + mathematics) is the statistical study of biological phenomena. In addition, the role of technology has greatly contributed to both positive and negative changes within other fields. For instance, employment of individuals whose background is solely in mathematics is expected to decrease through 2008; however, those who also have backgrounds in related disciplines such as computer science and electrical engineering will have better job opportunities (Bureau of Labor Statistics). As different fields continue to overlap, what are some additional careers that you anticipate seeing in the future? How will advancement in technology impact the field(s) in which you are interested?

WHERE ARE THE JOBS?

Employment opportunities are available in the areas of research, health care, the outdoors, education, and more! Possible places to look include:

- Colleges and universities
- Computer service firms (i.e., Microsoft, Adobe, Xerox)
- Electronics and computer manufacturers (i.e., IBM, Honeywell, Apple)

- Aerospace and transportation equipment manufacturers (i.e., Boeing, General Motors, Ford)
- Energy systems firms (i.e., Lockheed–Martin)
- Chemical and pharmaceutical manufacturers (i.e., Dupont, Kodak)
- Financial firms (i.e., Citibank, Prudential, Solomon Brothers)
- Producers of petroleum products (i.e., Exxon, Texaco)
- Engineering research organizations (i.e., AT&T Laboratories, Bell Laboratories)
- Communication service providers (i.e., AT&T, GTE)
- Consulting firms
- Federal and state agencies and organizations (i.e., Department of Defense, Department of Energy, National Science Foundation, NASA)

It should be noted that the National Academy for the Sciences (1996) reports increasing numbers of scientists, mathematicians, and engineers are finding that their skills are most needed in the financial world. For example, over 14 percent of the firms recruiting graduates from the Massachusetts Institute of Technology (MIT) in 1995 were financial institutions.

Deciding on the Career That's Right for You!

Many questions should be considered when deciding on a career in science, mathematics, and technology. Some of these include:

1. What are your goals?
    Consider the following:
    a. Are you pursuing this career in the hope of making a great discovery or contribution to society?
    b. Are you eager to explore different theories or formulate your own?
    c. Do you hope to better educate others about science, mathematics, or technology in an effort to help shape public policy?
    d. What are your strengths and weaknesses?
2. What are some of the daily activities of the particular career?
    Consider the following:
    a. Will there be challenges and continual stimulation?

    b.   Are there a variety of activities available or is intense focus placed on a single project?

    c.   In what type of atmosphere would you be working?

    d.   To what degree will you work and interact with others?

    e.   What aspects of the job will be rewarding?

3.   What is the current and future job market for this career? Consider the following:

    a.   What was the personnel demand for this career five years ago?

    b.   What is the current demand?

    c.   What is the anticipated personnel demand for this career five years from now?

    d.   To what extent do other disciplines (i.e., technology) impact this career?

In evaluating different occupations, talk with your family, friends, teachers, and others. Ask questions about their respective jobs. Consider job shadowing someone in a science, mathematics, or technology career that interests you in order to gain a better understanding of the routines and tasks involved. Also, participate in a career day or job fair and pursue summer opportunities that expose you to a variety of practical experiences that allow you to gain a better understanding of the field in which you are interested. There are places within your community to consider working at as a volunteer or intern: hospitals, laboratories, industries, colleges and universities, zoos, museums, and banks to name a few.

There are many computer and self-assessment instruments that may assist you in finding a career best suited for your particular strengths and weaknesses; likes and dislikes. For example, the Strong Interest Inventory compares a person's interests with those of people employed in certain professions. Check with your school or college counselor for this and other such helpful tools.

CLASSES TO TAKE

Taking classes in science, math, and technology can start at an early age. Many school districts, libraries, museums, and postsecondary institutions offer noncredit classes, seminars, and programs for preschool, elementary and secondary youth. A few have been designed specifically for girls. To determine what is offered in your community and surrounding area check with the groups mentioned above. Also, encourage your daily/weekly newspaper to establish a calendar of activities to keep everyone informed about interesting workshops, classes, or exhibits in the community and to assist you in developing and enhancing your interests and abilities early in life through participating in such opportunities.

While in elementary school, be sure to checkout the opportunities offered by the Girls Scouts, Girls Life, 4-H Club, Future Farmers of America (FFA), and Campfire Girls. These organizations offer many opportunities in the fields of science, math, and technology. Your school may offer before- and after-school enrichment classes. Always take advantage of every opportunity to study as much as you can about your favorite interest in each. In middle school, begin to lay a firm foundation for the advanced classes in these three specific areas. A great example would be to study Algebra I in seventh or eighth grade to begin the precalculus math sequence in order to complete all of the higher-level courses in high school. If appropriate classes are not available in middle school, ask if you may go to the high school to attend those of interest to you or consider an independent study at home.

During high school take as many courses as your schedule permits. Also determine which courses in math, science, and technology you can take as electives. With more courses completed you will be a step ahead when you enroll in a postsecondary institution such as a community college, college, or university. When you are reviewing information on these institutions, be sure to note the courses needed for majors in these academic areas.

If your school does not offer the courses in which you would like to enroll, consult postsecondary schools in your geographic area. Many high schools have concurrent- or dual-enrollment policies under which you can be in high school and also take courses at the collegiate level. In some states, high school and college credit may be offered for the same course. For example, at the Texas Academy for Mathematics and Science at the University of North Texas, students complete the last two years of high school and the first two years of college concurrently by taking college courses taught by university faculty.

Correspondence and on-line courses may also be available to you. Be sure to consult with your guidance counselor for all of the possibilities. It is important to note that even though your interest may lie in science or technology, a solid foundation in mathematics is necessary in these areas.

During middle school and high school, there are a multitude of after-school, residential, and nonresidential summer programs in science, math, and technology specifically for girls and young women in addition to those for both genders. A few of these are described in the Resource Section of this book. These experiences afford learning and social experiences usually with students of similar interests and abilities.

In middle school you may also choose to take part in one of the regional talent searches offered through the Talent Identification Program at Duke University, the Center for Talent Development at John Hopkins University, the Center for Talent Development at Northwestern University, or the Rocky Mountain Talent Search at the University of Denver. Check with your school counselor to determine the regional talent search in which your state participates. Participation in a talent search affords you the opportunity to take an above-level test, either the SAT or ACT (normally designed for eleventh and twelfth graders). If you are currently scoring in the upper-ninetieth percentile of your grade level achievement tests, an above-level testing experience can help provide a more accurate picture of your strengths in certain areas. In addition, talent searches and their cooperative programs offer accelerated and enriching summer educational programs in a variety of content areas. Such programs can allow you to explore your interest areas in greater depth and complexity.

READ! READ! READ!

From an early age read as many books as possible involving women in science, math, and technology. Years ago, books about females in these areas were only written at the adult level, but now there are many great publications directed to students at all levels. For example, Chelsea House Publishers has many biographies of women in these fields written specifically for young readers. As you think about these girls and women of note, compare and contrast their accomplishments. At what age did each develop their specific interest? Did she have a mentor or a role model? Were there specific experiences that helped or hindered her progress? What inspiration did you derive from reading the book? Is there a quotation from each person that you will use as inspiration for general or specific areas and interests in your life? Are there some stories you would like to share with your friends, teachers, or parents? Our great list of inspiring stories is located in the back of this book. Check out your school or city library for copies. You may want to put a few of your selections on your birthday or holiday gift list. Happy reading, and pass your favorite ones on to your girlfriends.

INSTRUCTIONAL MATERIALS

Although current textbooks in science, math, and technology have been more proactive in depicting girls and women in these areas of study than those of a decade ago and are attempting to use less gender-specific language, there are many examples of gender bias in the current instructional materials at the elementary, secondary, and collegiate levels. Review your current books. Look at the illustrations and photographs and determine how you would change them. Do boys perform experiments while girls observe? Do girls clean the labs after the experiment has been conducted? Is a male at the chalkboard solving the mathematical equation? Count the pictures in the book. How many show only male students and teachers? What is each gender doing? How many times is a female depicted engaging in something productive, industrious, or creative? How many teachers are males? Females? We know there should be equal numbers of photos with positive role models for girls. Which gender is used the most? When videos, films, and CD-ROMs are used, check for the same balance!

SPECIAL CLUBS—A GREAT IDEA!

There are situations in which girls feel more at ease only with their female friends and peers. Research indicates we are more interactive and perhaps concentrate better when boys are not in classes, especially in science, math, and technology classes. Noncompetitive situations with the other gender sometimes bring out our nurturing nature with our female friends. Some schools have all-girl courses, but most do not. If you think it would be a good idea in your school, talk to your guidance counselor and principal.

You may want to ask some of your friends to go with you. Remember presenting facts works to your advantage rather than just speaking in generalizations. If it is not possible to take special courses, do not be shy or hesitate to ask your teacher for help. Teachers, male or female, sometimes have a tendency to call on boys more than girls. Let them be aware of what you know and if you have questions.

You could even organize a special group or club and meet during lunch or after school to share and discuss similar interests. A good way to gather resources would be to meet at the local library to determine the books, videos, and CD-ROMs on topics that interest your club. Perhaps your members have mothers, other female family members, or friends who are involved in careers in science, math, and technology. Ask them to join you at one of your meetings. Being together in a club will be fun, but more important, you will learn a lot.

FINDING A MENTOR

A mentor is a person who shares guidance and instruction and can provide you with additional experiences and knowledge related to your particular field of interest. In selecting the type of mentor that you would like to work with, consider the following:

- What do you want to learn more about?
    Perhaps you want to learn more about a particular career in mathematics, science, or technology. Or maybe you are interested in conducting or participating in a research project.
- What are your transportation considerations?
    You may need to discuss the possibility of getting rides or taking public transportaion with your parents before deciding on a mentorship.
- Do you have the time and are you willing to devote the time to a mentorship?
    Examine your current schedule to determine the days and times you can devote to a mentorship. Keep in mind that you will also have to consider your mentor's busy schedule.
- How long do you expect to be involved in the mentorship?

Some mentorships last a few weeks or a summer, others may last for years. Determine the type you prefer.

- Where might I find a mentor?

    There are many places within your community in which to find a mentor. Colleges and universities, businesses and industries, organizations and associations are just a few places to consider.

- How can I stay safe?

    Involve your parents, a teacher, or school or college counselor in your mentor search. Perhaps they know individuals who would make excellent mentors. Always meet with your new mentor in a public place with other people present or take a friend, parent, or teacher with you until you feel comfortable. Younger girls may always want to have a familiar adult accompany them.

While expertise and skill in a particular area is an important characteristic of good mentors, they must also be eager to share their knowledge and they should be patient, especially when working with young children. Good communication and flexibility are also qualities that should be considered when selecting a mentor. You may want to develop a list of questions to ask potential mentors so that you can pick the individual who will best meet your needs and fulfill what you have in mind for your mentorship.

Technology has helped to enhance mentorships. E-mail and faxing can help alleviate the need to travel. If you live in a small, rural area or have transportation restrictions, technology can bring the mentoring experience right into your home or school. Furthermore, by using technology your "pool" of potential mentors is expanded.

It is important when initiating a mentorship that you and your mentor establish a plan. How often will you meet? What are your mutual goals? What do each of you hope to gain from the overall experience? Clearly communicate to your mentor what you hope to gain from the experience. Additionally, a final product or culminating activity resulting from the experience should be considered, for example, how will the knowledge and skills gained from the mentorship be shared and communicated with others?

Part II

STORIES OF

ACCOMPLISHMENT

G irls and young women have made many extraordinary accomplishments in science, mathematics, and technology. You will find inspiration in the amazing stories that follow. As you read, take note of the challenges they faced, the individuals who encouraged them along the way, and the goals they have set for their futures.

Some of the terminology used by these girls may be unfamiliar since the girls are speaking with the voices of the scientists, mathematicians, and technologists that they are! We encourage you to research any unfamiliar terms that you are interested in learning more about.

In addition, it should be noted that each of these young women has selected to discuss a particular aspect of the process she has gone through to achieve her goals. Some have discussed their research in great detail; others have recalled a particular moment when they realized where their true passion lay.

You will notice that several of the following stories are from girls who have attended the Hathaway Brown School in Ohio. The nature of this school has afforded these young women some extraordinary research opportunities that are especially worthy of noting.

YOUNG WOMEN OF
ACHIEVEMENT

Ages
Eighteen
and Younger

Cristen Andrews

Alexandra Breedlove

Lindsey Cameron

Rebecca Davis

Kaitlin Fairweather

Bonnie Colleen Gurry

Ann Lai

Laura Marx

Nicole Nole

Elina Onitskansky

Callie Pfeiffer, Ashli Pfeiffer, Maggie Kelley, Sabrina Kelley

Ashlee Riddle

Andeliz Sanchez Roman

Amy Beth Saltzman

Kyra Sedransk

Jennifer Seiler

Jackie Swanson

Evelina Alicia Teran

Hallie Lynn Woodward

Erica Elizabeth Youngstrom

CRISTEN
ANDREWS

*C*risten Andrews was born August 16, 1983, in Austin, Texas. She lives with her mother, Tamra; her father, Carlton; her younger sister, Carolyn; a big, loveable German shepherd; and four cats. She currently attends Westlake High School in Austin where she is an active member of the band and several other organizations, including Spanish Club, Culture Club, and Amnesty International. She has always enjoyed music and plays both the clarinet and the bass guitar. Her favorite subjects are English, Spanish, and photojournalism.

YOUNG AVIATOR

I don't know when I decided that I wanted to learn how to fly, but I first developed an interest while seeing the Blue Angels at an air show with a friend. As I watched the planes do spins and loops through the air, the thought of flying a plane thrilled me. I liked the loud noise, the high altitudes, and the idea of doing something most people never have the chance to do.

Now that I have started flying lessons, my dream to fly seems more like an accomplishment than an intangible goal. I know that if it weren't for my parents' help, however, I wouldn't have even gotten this far. It costs a lot of money to learn how to fly, but because I intend to pursue flying as a career, it seems worth the money. It also seems worth the time and effort. I take flight lessons about once every two weeks, driving an hour north of Austin to a small airport in Georgetown that houses several flight training schools and rents airplanes. Between lessons, I spend quite a bit of time preparing. Before I started flying I had to purchase a lot of materials from a huge list—materials that ranged from an airport directory and a flight maneuvers manual to a flight computer, a fuel quantity indicator, and headphones. I also purchased a huge stack of books that I'm expected to read in order to pass the test to get my license. Every couple of lessons, I receive a video that outlines key concepts presented to me in the chapter. It takes an enormous amount of hard work and dedication to learn how to fly. Learning about aviation is like learning a new language—you have to master a completely new vocabulary and understand the science and math skills that pertain to it.

Memorizing words and reading books is just the beginning of the process of flight training, however. You have to then get into the aircraft and apply everything you've learned from the books. Taking notes and jotting down steps for basic flight procedures, such as steep turns and stalls, helps a great deal. However, as soon as you jump in a plane and have to recall them from memory, it isn't quite so simple. Not only do you have to learn to make decisions quickly, but you also have to perform multiple tasks simultaneously. There's not much room for mistakes once you're in the air, and if something does happen, you have to be able to identify what the problem is and know how to recover from it.

Fortunately, I have a great flight instructor. For the most part, he lets me do things on my own and only gives me advice if he feels I could use the help. Patience is something a flight instructor definitely needs to have. If my instructor didn't have the patience to deal with all the mistakes I have made, I don't know where I would be right now! Learning to fly a plane is a lot like learning to drive a car. Each training plane has dual controls, so even though I have the responsibility of operating my own controls, I have the comfort of knowing that if something were to happen, the instructor would use his controls to guide the plane to a safe recovery. My instructor is great at talking me through the flight procedures and reinforcing what I've already learned. At this point in my training, he remains beside me during the flights. But even though I do have the instructor beside me in the air, it is my responsibility to fly the plane. Flying demands that pilots become independent, and that's one of the things I like most about it.

Of course, it takes a lot of preparation and training to become confident and capable enough to be independent. It takes more than simply studying the controls. I have to learn the proper way to check that the equipment is safe for flight.

A typical flight lesson begins with some time in the classroom where we go over what I read, outline basic ideas, and talk in detail about the goals for the upcoming flight. Then we go out to the aircraft and look for the necessary aircraft documents, check the oil and make sure the instruments will be working properly in the air, and adjust the aircraft so that it will be able to support the weight of the flight. We call and get a weather report, verify the wind direction, and determine the runway we will use. All the check lists and radio calls take a long time and seem monotonous at first, but making sure everything is working accurately is essential. Safety is extremely important, and as a pilot, you are expected to know when the conditions are safe to fly as well when they aren't.

I suppose that when I first thought about flying, I had no idea how much was involved in the process of becoming a pilot. It's important to understand all the technical terms and scientific theories because they explain why a plane flies in the first place. What I did know was that I would love the feeling of taking the plane up into the air and soaring through the sky with the clouds beneath me. That feeling alone makes all the hard work worth the effort. It even makes it fun. The books I read are technical, and some of the subject matter is extremely difficult, but I know that understanding it is all part of becoming a good pilot. I want to be a great pilot. That makes reading the technical books more of a pleasure than a pain.

I have been flying planes now for a little over six months, and I am well on the way to soloing. My first solo flight will be both exciting and scary, but I feel confident that I'll be prepared. I know, too, that if I do well, I'll be even more excited about getting my pilot's license. Once I get my license, I hope to be able to work as a flying instructor so that I can continue to learn, teach, and earn money while I build up the necessary hours to become a private pilot. Then, after that, who knows? There are so many options, and lots of opportunities—especially for women. I'm not sure yet if I want to fly big planes or small planes, or if I want to work as a corporate pilot or a charter pilot. But any job that involves flying planes, traveling, and getting paid to do it sounds good to me. I love to fly. I love the feeling of being so high in the sky. It's great to feel so free!

ALEXANDRA
BREEDLOVE

*A*lexandra Breedlove was born on August 12, 1984, the second of two children. She is a native of Cleveland Heights, Ohio. She is currently a junior at Hathaway Brown School in Shaker Heights, Ohio. Until the fall of 1999, she was a dedicated figure skater, skating in the mornings before school and sometimes after school and on weekends. In the summer of 1998, she began her current passion, basketball. She continues to play year-round for the school team. Her favorite subjects have always been math and science. She is a very hardworking and dedicated student with a logical and analytical mind.

BONE RESEARCH

In eighth grade, I conducted a science fair project on the strength of different building materials. I dropped a weight on wood and different kinds of metals and used a video camera and a ruler to determine how much each deflected. I was interested in this because I knew almost nothing about the strength of building materials and wanted to expand my knowledge. After signing up for a class at school called "research seminar," my teacher asked me what type of project I would like to participate in. After much consideration and some help from my teacher, I decided I wanted to do something similar to my project the previous year, combining math and science. Through her many contacts, she found a project with the perfect blend of engineering and biology working in the Orthopedic Engineering Lab at Case Western Reserve University under the supervision of Dr. Clare Rimnac. Dr. Rimnac is an associate professor in the Department of Mechanical and Aerospace Engineering. At our first meeting, she suggested two different projects. The first was to work with her on hip and knee implant research. The second was to work with a graduate student on bone strength and mechanics. I chose the second project because I felt that working with the actual bone would be more interesting, but I was not sure what either was exactly, so it was more of a blind choice.

The second time we met, I learned more about the structure of bone and its many components. After I knew more about bone structure, I would begin working on the project. I met with the graduate student who was already well into the project. The first few times I went to the lab, I did busy work, such as making dyes and plastics that we eventually used to embed in the bones. I was bored with these talks, thinking there must have been something more challenging for me to do than measure different substances and mix them together. Of course, there was, but they could not immediately give me the responsibility to use hundred of dollars worth of equipment until I knew what I was doing. At the time, I did not understand this, but now that I have the opportunity to work with the expensive equipment, I know exactly why they did not let me use it at first. Working with this equipment is difficult, even if you know what you are doing and especially if you do not.

That summer, the summer before I began my sophomore year, I began working on the actual project. We were trying to find out how much weaker radiated bone is than regular bone. Bones are radiated to sterilize them for bone implants, or allografts. It is crucial to radiate bones to reduce the chances for disease, but it significantly reduces bone strength. We knew this from the start, but we were trying to find out how much it reduces bone strength and resistance to fracture under stress. We sectioned the bones into small rectangular pieces with a small notch cut partway into the bone to guide the start of the crack. We tested the bone samples on a large screw-driven machine that slowly pulled the specimen apart, causing it to slowly crack down the center. We determined how much force has to be applied to the bones to cause them to break in half. We also had sensors attached to the bones to "listen" for small cracks that form around a larger crack to help relieve the pressure put on the bone. We found that the radiated bones were 56 percent easier to break than the normal bones. This means that if, during a bone transplant, a surgeon chips the bone with one of his tools, it will fracture much more easily and more quickly than a regular bone would with a similar chip.

I took this project to the Northeast Ohio Science and Engineering Fair held at Cleveland State University in the spring of 2000. I placed third in my category. In addition, Case Western Reserve University submitted the work to two medical journals, both of which accepted the work. This year, I am working on another project through the same department. We are testing age-related differences in bone composition and strength. I will be testing the density of bones on my own for this experiment. I learned that although I did not get to do challenging things at the beginning, I am doing things now that I never thought were possible.

The bone-strength experiment taught me so much about the field of science research and about myself. I learned that you have to follow through with something you begin, no matter how much you do not want to because it probably will get better. And even if it does not, you can take away so much from the experience. In my case, I did not quit at the beginning and later realized the importance of the work I was doing. I also learned from the experience. I realized that most people spend years doing easy things and learning the basics before beginning an experiment. I was lucky because I only had to wait a few months. I also learned the importance of responsibility and dedication. If you are going to accomplish what seems impossible, you cannot ever give up. I learned that sometimes research starts slow. You have to write grants, find out all the information you need, find quality materials, write a procedure, and practice techniques before beginning the experiment. This has helped me in all aspects of my life.

This past summer, while working on my new project with a different graduate student, we ran into many obstacles. Many of the machines we needed to use were no longer in the lab, and many of the materials we needed were difficult to get. We had to do research and search for different ways to do things. We had to make new contacts and find old ones. We had to wait for responses and for others, who said we could use their equipment, to follow through with their promises. To overcome these obstacles, we worked hard together to find all the information we needed, and when we finally had all the pieces, we put them together to begin the project quickly and smoothly.

If I could do something like this over again, knowing all the good and bad aspects, I definitely would. In fact, as I said before, I am. I began the new project this past summer and have used everything I learned in the past to guide me through this one. It has been the best experience of my life. I have learned so much and found out things I never thought were possible. I realize that many people do not have opportunities like this until they are much older, and I realize how lucky I am. When I tell people about my project, most are shocked to learn what I have been working on. I never truly realized the extent of this opportunity until I heard others' reactions.

I would advise other girls to take any opportunity they can get. The smallest project or idea could turn into the next new invention or the next big breakthrough. Never give up. Never wonder what you could have done better. Try your hardest. Give everything you have to your commitments. Other people are counting on you. But, more important, it feels great to know that your accomplishments might make someone else's life easier or better. Always remember that you are lucky and special. No matter who you are, you can make a difference, no matter how many people tell you that you cannot. Also, you can always change your situation. If you know you can do more, tell someone. Do not ever be content with something that does not challenge you. Always give yourself the opportunity to test your limits and to find new talents. Respect people who deserve it, but do not be afraid to tell them your ideas. Take pride in your accomplishments. Most people are astonished to find what you can do. Most important, have fun with what you do.

LINDSEY DENISE
CAMERON

ℒindsey Denise Cameron was born February 11, 1984, in Chicago to Jake and Denise Cameron. She attends the Texas Academy of Mathematics and Science, a program that allows talented high school students to complete the last two years of high school and the first two years of college simultaneously. Even though she enjoys the closeness of her friends in her dorm, she misses her parents; her siblings, Ryan, Courtney, and Sydney; her Aunt Peggy Sue; and her giant Shiloh shepherd, Triton. Lindsey's favorite classes are calculus and the materials science research class. Her interests include human rights, tennis, and collecting pictures of '40s movie stars.

POLYMER LIQUID CRYSTALS

Being slightly abnormal has always been normal for me. I breezed through school, skipping grades, winning numerous awards and teachers' praise. I

41

always felt underchallenged, bored, and outside my social group, so during my freshman year of high school, I was looking for a change.

During the summer of my freshman year, I found an article about the Texas Academy of Mathematics and Science (TAMS). It is a school for high school students who complete the last two years of high school and the first two years of college simultaneously. Students take a math- and science-based curriculum at the University of North Texas for two years. The academy promised to be a solution for students bored in high school. I fit the basic criteria and became fascinated by my new options.

I dedicated myself to being accepted and later excelling at TAMS. The academy became the focal point of my sophomore year because of its numerous opportunities. This experience would allow me to interact with different people and let me be the first person in my family to undertake a Bachelor of Science degree or even go to college.

I investigated the fields of math and science during that summer to see if I would be compatible with the academy. After a lot of work, I built my own computer and found computer engineering to be an area I relished. I also became intrigued by chemistry, thanks to an awesome chemistry teacher. Books about nuclear chemistry and quantum physics were devoured as I read about quarks, neutrinos, and other subunits of the atom. I developed a fascination for both computer engineering and molecular chemistry. My overwhelming passion in those subjects helped me finalize my decision to apply to the academy and be successful there.

The application process involved gathering essays and teachers' recommendation letters. I was eager to tell my friends all about TAMS, but every time negative criticisms were encountered, such as: "Why do you want to leave high school early?" "What about prom, yearbooks, and football games?" "Won't you miss your friends?" and the most repeated "Don't grow up too soon!" It hurt that my friends gave little support for something that I believed in and valued. Even though my friends showed little support, my family supported all my endeavors; without them I could never have achieved what I have today.

My parents' only concern was my mathematical background. During my sophomore year, I focused on understanding math concepts and retaught myself algebra. My family supported and encouraged me throughout.

When my acceptance letter came from TAMS, I was elated and ecstatic, literally screaming and jumping at the mailbox. I felt as if a chapter in my life was closing and a new one was beginning.

I excitedly spent my summer preparing for the academy and learning more about computers. I was a computer intern for the American Red Cross. I learned about computer engineering, its applications, troubleshooting, and interacting with a variety of people. One afternoon, though, I started contemplating TAMS and all it encompassed. I was leaving my family, friends, and comforts of home at the impressionable age of fifteen. Not many average teenagers would take this challenge. For the first time, I began to listen to my friends' advice and began to fear I had taken on too much. Because of my dreams and dedication to my family, I reevaluated my fears and decided I wouldn't turn down an opportunity like TAMS.

I had goals of emulating my role model, Madame Curie, who discovered three periodic elements, won two Noble Prizes, and was the first woman in Europe to receive her doctorate. I plan to be the first woman in my family with a college degree and the first person in that same family to earn a Ph.D., while aspiring to make radical changes like Madame Curie.

I entered the Texas Academy of Mathematics and Science in the fall of 1999. I have bonded with many people here. My friends and I have had many diverse conversations ranging from philosophy to religion to quantum physics. While at TAMS I have become active in human rights and been able to dive into my passion of chemistry and computers.

The activity that gives me the most pleasure is my research. I just finished an eight-month project in the Materials Science and Engineering Department at the University of North Texas studying polymers, a component of plastic.

Imagine it's a cold morning and the car won't start. After consulting with a costly mechanic, the mechanic determines that the polymer that keeps the gasket fluids from leaking into the engine has deformed because of the cold and has caused considerable damage. My area of research is to prevent these costly errors. Since polymers are integral to industry, knowing their reactions to temperature is pertinent. I determined the beta transition, a temperature region where a polymer's properties change, for a polymer blend. I used mathematical and experimental components in my research.

Polymers are incorporated into plastics because of their chemical resistance, low flammability, and ease of processing. Unfortunately, at different temperatures polymers change their structure because of the addition of heat. By using a computer-animated program called Scilab, I applied a tensile form to a polymer and determined when and where the polymer broke. By knowing when the polymer breaks, engineers can properly add reinforcements to the polymer so it won't break.

My main area of research was an independent project. I worked forty hours a week for three months determining at what temperature a polymer's structure reorders; this can lead to crack propagation. I studied the beta transition of polymers by using Dielectric Analysis (DEA). DEA is a new field of research in the laboratory of Dr. Witold Brostow that applies an oscillating frequency and heat to a sample. By knowing the beta transition, we can deduce the material's properties at any temperature. It is pertinent to know the beta transition in designing missiles, manufacturing prosthetics, or developing microelectronics. A chemical company is currently using my results to design and manufacture intraocular lenses.

Based on my research this summer, I have applied for the Intel Science Talent Search and Barry M. Goldwater Scholarship. I was also selected to teach a graduate class, Methods of Thermal and Electrical Analysis of Polymers, will speak at the POLYCHAR World Forum on Polymer Applications and Theory, and recently spoke at the Latino Conference of Science and Technology: Beyond 2001.

I enjoy materials science and engineering research because it is a frontier in science and has many practical applications. In my lab we are working on building safer, more efficient plastics. This research has the potential to impact many industries as polymers and liquid crystals can be used in everything from bulletproof vests to microelectronics packaging to optical devices.

Applied mathematics is also intriguing. Math is powerful and the foundation of nearly every application. I am currently conducting a calculus project to calculate the functions of stock prices. In this area I have grown to appreciate mathematics and also correlate abstract mathematics to practical uses.

I intend to take my enjoyment of working hands on with computers and complex data and apply it to a major in computer/electrical engineering or computer science at a four-year university. Ultimately my goal is to work with the government in high-tech fields such as cryptology or signal analysis.

Even though my decision to leave high school early is not average, I feel comfortable and secure in my choice. TAMS has not only allowed me great research opportunities in my field of interests but, more important, the chance for interaction with a variety of people. Succeeding here is my biggest accomplishment, because it takes courage and dedication. The TAMS experience not only ties into my future career goals but also teaches me valuable lessons in perseverance, teamwork, and ingenuity that will last me a lifetime.

REBECCA
DAVIS

*R*ebecca Davis was born February 27, 1987. She lives with her parents and seventeen-year old brother in Mississippi. Rebecca is involved in many school activities at Picayune Junior High School including student council, drama club, band (she plays the oboe), and the gifted program. She is also a dancer and hopes to be on the dance team in high school. In sixth grade, Rebecca won second place at her school's science fair with the project titled "Planetary Magnetic Fields." She also received the special achievement award from NASA at the regional science fair. She is very interested in science and hopes to attend medical school to be a psychiatrist someday.

THE MYSTERY OF THE MAGNETIC FIELD

"Hey Rebecca, remember last year when the school didn't let us have a science fair?" asked Jenny.

"Oh yeah. I wanted to do a project. I hope that I get to do one this year," I answered with a hopeful look on my face.

"Class. Class! CLASS!! Be quiet. I want to talk to you about the upcoming science fair. Everyone has to do a project. It doesn't have to be very hard project, but if you don't do a project, you get a zero for a test grade," explained our teacher, Mrs. Ladner.

Everyone in the class started talking. Some were talking with contentment and some with disappointment. Well . . . *almost* everyone was talking. I was sitting at my desk trying to think of a really good science project. I was trying to think of a science project that would show my intelligence as well as my hard work and determination.

At home that afternoon I talked with my family about what makes a good science project. The only advice they gave was to do a project using things in which I was interested. It took me a while to think of something, but I finally decided on something involving magnets and the earth. I knew it would be hard to come up with something that involved both things, but I was going to try.

I searched the Internet night after night until one day I discovered a Web site for kids that discussed a project relating to magnetic fields. Suddenly, I realized the earth has a magnetic field! The project on the Web involved using baby oil and steel shavings to show what magnetic fields looked like, but I couldn't use baby oil because there was a rule against having liquids at the science fair. This is what brought me to my next challenge. I had to find a substance that could act like water, but harden. It took me days to find such a thing, but I finally discovered an acrylic called Liquid Glass at a hobby store. Although my project was complete, I still had to study the science behind it so I could make a good presentation to the class.

At the school's science fair, I received second place in my category. One of the judges asked me many questions about my project. I was very proud to be able to answer them all correctly!

At the regional science fair, I was really nervous because I knew I would have to speak to many judges about my project. When I walked into the gym where the fair was being held, I saw hundreds of projects. I saw a lot of projects that looked so much better than mine. I soon realized that everyone at the science fair was just as nervous as I was.

Judges came around one at a time. It seemed like an eternity. Finally, a special judge came around, and I was asked some very hard questions. I was glad I hadn't listened to my friends when they told me I was studying too much!

Time passed and many kids became bored, but finally the judging was complete. While the judges added up their scores, we were allowed to leave for an hour. However, it was soon time to return to the gym for the awards ceremony.

I sat through the ceremony until the announcer came to my category. I was sitting on the edge of my seat hoping they would call my name. One by one the awards were given. I longed to hear my name called to receive an award, but that didn't happen. I fell back into my seat and felt as if tears were about to pour from my eyes. I started getting my things together when I heard the announcer say something about one more award still to be given. I decided to stay. The award was the Special Achievement Award from NASA for science and engineering. I didn't think anything of it and continued to get my things together. Then, I heard my name being called! I couldn't believe it! I received a very special award instead of *just* an award. I ran down the stairs and almost tripped. I made it to the bottom and was presented with a plaque and had a photo taken.

Winning the award changed me in a way I had not expected. I am no longer afraid to speak in public, and I have discovered my love for science and learning. I know that if more girls compete in science fairs, they will feel better about themselves because it will provide them with the power and the will to learn as well as teach.

KAITLIN
FAIRWEATHER

*K*aitlin Fairweather, known by family and friends as Kati, was born January 26, 1987, in Nashua, New Hampshire. She currently lives in Amherst, New Hampshire, with her older brother, Jim, and her mother and father. Most of Kati's time is focused on school. She likes her industrial arts class where she can be creative and make different things out of wood or metal. She also likes English.

After school, Kati is involved in sports. She plays field hockey and basketball for Amherst Middle School, as well as soccer, swimming, and lacrosse. Kaitlin is creative and open-minded, qualities which have helped her in the inventing process. She is also shy, which did not help! In her free time, Kati enjoys hanging out with her friends.

NO LOSS LACROSSE

My decision to pursue the science/math field was based on circumstance. I guess sometimes you are just in the right place at the right time, though I didn't know it then. In the sixth grade, part of our integrated curriculum was an invention unit. Every sixth grade student at Amherst Middle School had to participate in this invention unit. The idea of the unit is to make us think through the invention process. We had to come up with something novel and needed, keep daily journals, do research, apply some science and math knowledge, some marketing, manufacturing, and economics. We had to call companies, go online, send out letters, and so forth to make sure the idea for our invention was original. We then had to make a display complete with advertisements, product price, jingles, and a description of the process we used to make our gadget.

Reading books has been a favorite pastime of mine. Whether a novel, fantasy, or biography, I especially like stories about girls or women who have overcome adversity of some sort, or done something out of the ordinary and have been successful. I have been amazed at how women (and men) have invented products or processes, sometimes by chance, that changed our world. I, however, did not plan to invent anything so grandiose. In fact, my initial goal was to come up with something simple, doable, and inexpensive, get an A on my assignment, and be done.

I had trouble thinking of an invention at first. I come from a very athletic family, so I thought I could do something for sports. When I was going through the brainstorming process, thinking of all the sports I play and what was needed, I thought about lacrosse. There is no way to practice lacrosse by yourself, unless you have access to a brick wall with no windows. (My brother had already thrown a ball through our garage door, so that was off limits as a practice wall.) One big problem for me was our large backyard, bordered by a river, a field, and woods. Every year my brother and I set our lacrosse goal on the grass, but many lacrosse balls were lost while practicing shooting goals. We must have lost dozens in the river, the woods, or the field around our home, so most of our practice time was spent hunting for lacrosse balls. One sure way to end practice is to lose the last ball, and lacrosse balls are expensive to keep replacing. This became my problem to solve: limiting the loss of lacrosse balls. This problem influenced my decision and inspired me to work toward a solution.

My invention is called NO LOSS LACROSSE. It is a twelve-foot piece of strong elastic cord. On one end of the cord is a metal clip that attaches to the strings on the top and backside of a lacrosse stick. On the other end of the cord is a Teflon-coated mesh bag. The cord is woven through the mesh bag, and a lacrosse ball is secured in the bag with a series of knots.

I wrote and called many lacrosse companies from around the country to see if there was a similar product on the market. From my responses, many companies said no, but several referred me to a product called Sololax. We owned a Sololax, so I knew what these companies were talking about, and I also knew that my product was not at all like it. Just to make sure, I wrote up a product comparison showing the differences between NO LOSS LACROSSE and Sololax. Our house seems to be on every lacrosse magazine mailing list, and I looked through many lacrosse catalogs and found nothing that was like my invention.

It was winter in New Hampshire when I took my invention out for a test. Because of all the snow, I ended up using it in my driveway. Not only did NO LOSS LACROSSE work for shooting a goal, it was great for practicing catching and throwing by yourself. It bounced back very quickly off the pavement. Suddenly my product had a much wider application, not only for shooting goals, but also for practicing basic skills without a teammate or a wall.

The first NO LOSS LACROSSE I made was with a strong, but thin elastic cord. I could shoot goals from thirty feet away and the elastic was only ten feet long. I gave it to a varsity lacrosse player from our high school to try. When he used it, the cord snapped. This was my first of many learning experiences. I got a thicker elastic cord, but the bounce back was too quick, and I knew inexperienced players would never be able to catch the ball. I lengthened this thicker elastic to twelve feet, and that solved the elastic problem and the bounce-back time.

Another obstacle I faced was the quality of the mesh bags. A couple of them ripped, and I learned that only the ones that were treated with Teflon were able to hold up on pavement. This meant I had to carefully inspect each bag before putting a ball in.

I finished my project in the six-week time frame, did my presentation, and received an A. I thought I was done. However, at the end of my presentation, several classmates asked if I would make one for them. They were willing to buy one at my $9.99 price! This figured to be a 50 percent profit for me!

I did receive an Honorable Mention ribbon for my work, but I did not win locally, nor did I get recommended to present my invention at the State Invention Convention. Having so many classmates interested in buying my invention, I asked my mom to talk to our local lacrosse club to see if I could sell NO LOSS LACROSSE at the Granite State Lacrosse

Jamboree, to be held in our town the following month. Over sixty teams from New England participate in this youth tournament.

My mom and I made seventy, packaged them, and added a liability waiver, which seems to be a necessity these days. It basically said to use NO LOSS LACROSSE carefully, away from other people, and to check the knots on the bag periodically. I sold them with a friend, Casey, and my brother, Jim. In just two hours they sold out, and a mailing list of other interested people had to be created. Selling was my least favorite part of the process. However, the kids who bought NO LOSS LACROSSE immediately opened them and started using them. These impromptu demonstrations became a great selling tool.

To update my project, my dad and a patent attorney have helped me file for both a patent and a trademark. Our local newspapers have written about my invention, and I have recently sold thirty more at our Town Youth Lacrosse registration for the upcoming season. My lacrosse-playing friends and cousins from Pennsylvania, California, and Colorado have also taken NO LOSS LACROSSE to their states. I have met with an executive of a major lacrosse company and we are looking at a licensing agreement. This company would market, manufacture, and sell my product exclusively, and I would receive a percentage for every one sold! What started as a simple idea filled a void in the youth lacrosse marketplace, a practice device that didn't require a teammate or brick wall or backboard.

During my invention process, it took a lot of courage for me to stand up, explain my invention, and then sell it, especially to people I didn't know. I tend to be a shy person; so selling was the hardest part of my business venture, and the part which I was most uncertain about in my invention process. Even with that uncertainty, I took a deep breath and did the best I could. I was amazed at what I achieved.

I learned many things from my invention experience about the cost of materials, labor, profit margins, quality, supply and demand, and how to sell with confidence. I also learned how one very simple idea can grow into a product that everyone wants. Listening to customers and other lacrosse business people, I received many good ideas about my product distribution. I would definitely do this again. It was fun and I did make money!

My female role models are my mom, my two grandmothers, and my friends. All of them supported and encouraged me to keep going after the initial project was complete. The advice I would give to others is if you believe in your idea, work to make it the best you can, and listen to others who may have suggestions. Anything is possible. Don't necessarily use all of the suggestions you receive, stay true to your product or idea. Be willing to take some risks. Believe, step forward, and your self-confidence will follow.

BONNIE COLLEEN
GURRY

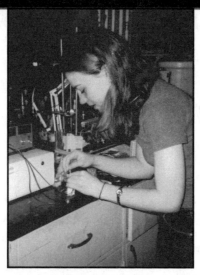

*B*onnie Colleen Gurry was born May 27, 1984, to Mel and Marilyn Gurry of Cleveland, Ohio. She has an older sister, Mary Bridget. Her elementary school years were spent at a small Catholic School before she transferred to Hathaway Brown School, a girls' junior and senior high school. While she is very close to many of her neighbors, Bonnie often finds herself roaming throughout Cleveland and its suburbs to get together with friends and family. Because the importance of reading and education has been enforced from the time she was very young, it is important to Bonnie to be constantly learning new things and having new experiences. These ideals play a role not only in her academics, but also in other aspects of her life as well.

MICROSENSOR INVENTION

When I started high school at Hathaway Brown, I was offered the opportunity to participate in the Research Seminar Program. This program, headed by my mentor Mrs. Patty Hunt, sets girls up with scientists and professionals throughout the Cleveland area. Through Mrs. Hunt, I was introduced to Dr. C. C. Liu of Case Western Reserve University. Dr. Liu heads the Edison Sensor Technology Center, which is one of the world leaders in the field of microelectrochemical sensors. Dr. Liu offered me and two other girls the chance to design and create our very own sensor. Realizing how lucky I was, I immediately said yes, despite the fact that I had no clue what a microsensor was, how it worked, or how I would try to use it.

The first step of my project actually was one of the hardest for me. I had to choose what my sensor would detect. This was especially difficult because there was practically no limit on what I could choose, and there was no one who could tell me what to do. So, after many weeks of deliberation, I settled upon a sensor that would monitor and control chlorine levels in a pool or spa. I honestly don't remember the exact thought process that brought this idea to me, but it wasn't an easy one. I was partially inspired by bitterness resulting from my parents' constant rejection of any sort of pool at our house, citing the difficulty of maintaining one. Simultaneously, my school swim team's practice was canceled after it was discovered that the chlorine levels were too high to swim in. After being convinced that my idea was feasible, I set upon the task of creating the actual sensor, which was yet another grueling process at times.

There have been many, many times when I definitely wanted to give up. Not necessarily because of difficulty with what I was doing, but more to do with my fleeting attention that every teenager often faces. Also, there were tons of times when I had no idea what I was doing. It was at these times that I had to trust those around me to help and guide me along the way.

The most important thing that I learned from this project is that no matter how hard something sounds, everything is doable. Although you don't simply arrive at your goal overnight, it is possible to achieve it. I learned that to everything, even the impossible task of creating a sensor, there is a process. Through a process, any difficult task is broken down into manageable steps that anyone can manage. People don't believe me when I say that anyone can do what I did, but it's true. With support, guidance, and perseverance, everyone has the ability to accomplish a goal, no matter how hard it may seem.

One of the main reasons why people think what I did was impossible is because they assumed that I did it alone. Under no circumstances was this invention something that I came up with in my basement by myself. First of all, I had the constant support of my advisor, Mrs. Hunt. She kept me on track and focused. Then there was Dr. Liu and all of his staff. Originally he was the one who I worked with the most. When he first sat me down and asked me, "So what do you want to do?" I was a little overwhelmed. But, he showed me that the project could be done in steps. Then he did what all good teachers do: he let go. While I continued to learn techniques and processes from others in his lab such as Laura Dudik or Mrs. Shao, I was essentially on my own. At first it frustrated me that he knew the answers to my questions, yet refused to answer them, telling me: "That is what you are going to find out!" which did nothing to ease my aggravation. However, I am now beginning to realize that I have learned much more from this method than I would have, had someone been holding my hand.

Since I have started this project, I have halfheartedly entered several local science fairs. I have had some success; however, because they are not the main priority of my project, I do not focus on them too heavily. I have also begun the process of patenting my invention. In order to secure my rights to the idea, through the help of my school, I have filed a provisional patent, and I will file the actual patent soon. I have received larger benefits from my invention than pieces of paper or acknowledgments. First of all, I have gotten a taste of life, not only at a college level, but also at the professional level. I have had the opportunity to witness the brilliant minds of many different people and have learned to work with others who are from different backgrounds and professions. I have also gained insight from my project. It has taught me valuable organizational and planning skills.

If I had to do everything over again, I would still jump at this opportunity. I am more than lucky to have been given this chance, and I would do it again if the occasion arose.

ANN
LAI

*A*nn Lai was born to Dr. Chun-Liang and Mrs. Su-Jane Lai June 19, 1984, in Cleveland, Ohio; her brother Alec, is nine years old. Having moved to Taiwan after birth, Ann returned to America during third grade. She currently resides in Beachwood, Ohio, and attends Hathaway Brown School, where she is the newspaper copy editor, the TEAMS (Test of Engineering Aptitude, Mathematics, and Science—an academic competition) captain, the Asian Awareness Association president, the ski club coordinator, and a Model United Nations/Congress participant. She also organizes the Youth Tzu-Chi Organization, Cleveland Chapter, for community/international services. In addition to doing scientific research, she enjoys playing violin, swimming, skiing, snowboarding, reading, and writing poetry. Moreover, she loves art and takes an abstract art independent study and Chinese painting/calligraphy class. She is responsible and determined, always striving for perfection and giving her work her undivided attention. Most important, she takes risks, learns from experiences, and pushes limits, always seeking to better the world.

MONITORING SULFUR DIOXIDE EMISSIONS

I have always been interested in math and science. From an early age, I would try to build new gadgets for special purposes and draw elaborate designs for cars that could swim and fly. I was fascinated by bubble experiments with soaps and shampoos, by chemical reactions from mixing kitchen ingredients, and by the light refracted in different glassware. Since then, science has been a part of my life, and I see it as an old friend. I know it well, but there are always more pieces to the puzzle to find and to fit into the picture.

My female role models—besides my mother for her inner and outer beauty and for her patience, common sense, and self-sacrifice—are Madam Curie and Fa Mulan. I admire Marie Curie for her brilliance, her perseverance, and her dedication to her studies. In a sense, she died for her research on radiation. Furthermore, she was the first woman to win a Nobel Prize in science, and she was independent and strong. On the other hand, Fa Mulan is the main character of an old Chinese legend in which she, the daughter, went to war in the place of her elderly father, who was drafted, and survived. To me, she was the epitome of strength, individuality, determination, and selflessness. She was willing to take risks, to push the limits of society, and to challenge the social customs for her beliefs and for her family. Although she is not a scientific figure, to me she symbolizes the values needed for anyone to succeed in any field. I look to her in times of hardship and challenges.

In middle school, I started dabbling in scientific research. In eighth grade, I studied how porosity and thickness affect the permeability of water through different matrices. I designed my own testing apparatus and performed the experiment on my kitchen table. Finding the experience fun but somehow not complex enough in ninth grade, I moved on to researching in laboratories at the local Case Western Reserve University (CWRU), studying how the angle of inclination of finned and flat aluminum plates affected the heat transfer coefficients. This time I worked under my dad, learning everything from thermocouples to elaborate equations.

Enthralled with the atmosphere of the advanced laboratories and loving the independent exploration of the scientific work, I returned to the laboratory at the end of my freshman year. During freshman chemistry, I learned about the environmental damage caused by acidic deposition. Through more research, I found that these deposits were caused predominantly by sulfur dioxide, which remains unable to be monitored continuously and realistically. Eventually, I discovered that a department at CWRU focused on the new technology of electrochemical microsensors. I thought that if such technology could be used for sulfur dioxide, its emissions could be monitored and controlled, thus helping to reduce acidic deposition. I have always been an independent child and teenager, undaunted in the face of obstacles. So, upon deciding what I wished to pursue, I contacted Dr. C.C. Lui, chairman of the department. After researching further and composing a proposal, I met again with Dr. Lui, a wonderful and generous mentor, who approved my project. After two to three years of hard work and incessant research, design, and testing, I eventually developed a microsensor system capable of monitoring the level of sulfur dioxide in emissions and able to trigger a corrective process when the sulfur dioxide exceeds a certain level. With this system, sulfur dioxide emissions from anywhere can be easily and cheaply (approximately nine dollars per microsensor) monitored and controlled, and acidic deposition can be restrained and even reduced.

From my invention, I have obtained many benefits. There are the obvious benefits from winning first place at international competitions, to having a patent pending with the U.S. Patent Office, from being invited to the Worldwide Young Researchers for the Environment in Germany as part of EXPO2000, to being inducted into the National Gallery for America's Young Inventors that year. However, through this experience, I have also had the privilege of working with the brilliant Dr. Lui, an expert in microsensor technology, as well as others at CWRU.

Furthermore, I'm grateful to my parents and brother for always giving me the benefit of the doubt and waiting in the car in the snow for me to finish late-night experiments. I have also learned more about life and about how everyone makes mistakes. I have had sensor wires melt last minute, resulting in the need to start over completely. I have had machines break down just before deadlines and had delayed gas arrivals when the gas was crucial to further research. Through all these exasperating times, I have discovered my own strength to persevere, my own determination to improve whatever it is I do, my ability to learn from mistakes, and my willingness to dedicate myself to a cause until the end, no matter the risks I need to take or the limits I need to push.

Overall, this was an amazing experience of not only scientific invention, but also self-exploration. I have learned more about life and my own strengths. Overcoming obstacles, I have grown and matured. I have experienced the excitement of inventing something new, something of my imagination, just like I always dreamed as a child. I made my childhood dreams a reality—inventing something new for a special purpose to help the world and its people. If I ever had the option to relive this experience, I would immediately be willing to reexperience the journey without any alterations. This is because I loved every up and every down, every moment of action and every moment of waiting, every smile cracked and every tear shed during the experience. It is all of these melted and twisted together that taught me so much about life and about myself and made the experience so fulfilling.

In conclusion, I would advise anyone with any interest to do the following: Pursue all your interests and test each option out to see which one you most prefer. Always do something you love, something that interests you, and, once you decide on a project, never quit. Persevere and challenge the obstacles in your way. Stand up for your beliefs, your passions, yourself. There will be hard times, and there may be short-term failure; however, in the end, the success will be worth all the pain.

LAURA

MARX

*L*aura Marx was born in Cleveland, Ohio, on December 29, 1984, and has lived there all her life. She has an older brother and a younger sister. A sophomore at Hathaway Brown School, science and English are her favorite subjects. Her biggest activities outside of school are running and theater. She participates in both cross-country and track, and enjoys acting in school plays. Through the Hathaway Brown Science Research Seminar, she was given the opportunity to join the Polymer Erosion and Contamination Experiment (PEACE) team, which is a group of students working with NASA scientists to fly an experiment on both the space shuttle and the International Space Station. She has a desire to learn and succeed that helps her in all aspects of her life, including science.

POLYMERS IN SPACE

When I became a new student at Hathaway Brown School, I was excited to be free from the routine that had dominated my life for eight years of grade school. There were many opportunities that I could take advantage of in my new school. One of these was the Science Research Seminar, which had attracted me to Hathaway Brown in the first place. In it, high school girls like me are matched with scientists to perform research at places like the Cleveland Clinic and Case Western Reserve University. One project that interested me was the PEACE project. It was a group of students who were working with scientists at NASA to fly an experiment on the space shuttle and the International Space Station. I have always enjoyed reading, and one of the genres I find the most exciting is science fiction. I have read many stories set in the future, when traveling through outer space is as easy as traveling through your backyard. There were not any particular books that inspired me to join the project, but reading science fiction allowed me to see the unlimited possibilities we have in the future. Space travel fascinated me, and as I learned about the project, I realized the results really would give us important information that could be used for space travel. This was a very exciting project, so I joined the team. The only real doubt I had about joining was that I would not have enough time to devote to it. I was very busy with school, sports, and drama, but I realized this was an opportunity I should not pass up.

I had a lot to learn as the newest team member. The problem that we are trying to help solve is that of atomic oxygen erosion and silicone contamination in low-Earth orbit. In low-Earth orbit, atomic oxygen atoms ram into space shuttles and satellites, actually causing them to erode. Silicone is usually used to cover space shuttles and satellites, but it doesn't protect very well from erosion. Pieces of silicone often break off and contaminate experiments on the shuttle. We are going to send forty different polymers into space on a shuttle and the International Space Station to see how they withstand atomic oxygen erosion. I spent much of the first year on the project getting acquainted with it and learning more about what I was doing. One of the things I helped work on was finding a consistent way to salt-spray polymer samples. Salt crystals are going to be sprayed on the polymers to protect them in certain spots. After being exposed to atomic oxygen, there will be little plateaus of protected polymer. Then we can measure how much of the polymer has been eroded. Another method of measuring the erosion will be to measure the mass of polymers before and after the flight.

We have learned many things at NASA and have been given many unique opportunities. We use microscopes and equipment that we wouldn't otherwise have the chance to use. Working with the NASA scientists is also something that we are really lucky to have the opportunity to do. Kim de Groh and Bruce Banks are the scientists who we work with the most. They are great because, even though they know so much more science than we students do, they treat us as an equal part of the team. I have learned so much about the details of our project and the problem of atomic oxygen erosion from them. They always take the time to explain things to us and make sure we know what is going on in the project. I have also learned a lot from working on a team. I think that working on a group like the PEACE team is very different from working on a project alone. It is really important to use teamwork and cooperate. It is also important to make sure that we stay friends since we have to work with each other so much. Going to NASA every Friday after school during the school year and every day for five weeks during the summer, I got to know the other girls on the team very well. We have gotten to the point where we are able to have a lot of fun while we work.

Another thing I learned from being on this team is the importance of patience. There is so much more that has to go into a project like this than just the actual science and experimentation. There is a massive amount of organization needed to keep the project running. It also takes a lot of time to get things ready, like the time required to punch out samples of different polymers. Sometimes it does get a little boring spending so much time punching polymers and doing paper work, but I think about the end result and I know it is all worth it. The polymers are being mounted on the International Space Station this summer. I am only a sophomore in high school this year, so I will still be involved in the postflight analysis of the samples. I am really glad to have the chance to work on both the preflight and postflight parts of the project.

I really enjoy working on the PEACE project. It takes a lot of time and commitment, but I still manage to fit in other activities that I enjoy. It is exciting to know that I am part of a group that is performing an experiment that will help find a solution to a significant problem. I realize how lucky I am to be a part of this. For a long time, women and girls were not encouraged to take part in scientific endeavors. Now it is much easier for us to pursue any career or hobby we want. My family has always supported my participation in the PEACE team. I have also had a lot of role models. My mother has always been a woman who I look up to. She is a wonderful person and a wonderful mother. In the world of science, I look up to all the women who work at NASA. They pursued science when it was not as acceptable as it is now, and they have succeeded. I would advise other girls not to worry about what other people think when choosing their activities and careers.

NICOLE

NOLE

*N*icole Nole was born May 28, 1984, in Chicago, Illinois, to Robert and Suzanne Nole. The family then moved to Kalamazoo, Michigan, so her parents could attend college. Living there between the ages of three and twelve, Nicky threw herself into school, gaining study habits from her parents. Living in a city dominated by soccer, Nicky chose to participate in Kalamazoo's soccer team at the age of seven. Along with joining the soccer team, Nicky also had a new family member. Her sister, Morgan, was born June 19, 1991. After nine years of living in Kalamazoo, Nicky's father was called to Chicago to become a firefighter. So, the family returned to her birthplace. At this time, she worked hard in school, especially math, and she has continued achieving in the area of mathematics ever since.

MARVELOUS MATHLETE

I gained a strong foundation for math and science through academically talented programs and a program called Avant Garde while attending a public school in Kalamazoo, Michigan. Through group activities, I learned to expand my common knowledge of ideas and how to listen to others in their pursuit of solutions. I gained my first introduction to higher math in sixth grade by taking prealgebra.

When my family relocated to Chicago, I attended a Catholic school, which was a totally new experience for me. Not only was the dress code different (I had to wear a uniform), but so was their math. In seventh grade I was starting algebra, while the rest of my class was just beginning prealgebra. Therefore, I attended algebra class with eighth graders, which was a very scary experience. Not only was I the new kid in school, but I was also the kid who went to math class with eighth graders. In order to fit this adjustment into my schedule, I had one order of classes on Mondays, Wednesdays, and Thursdays and another for Tuesdays and Fridays.

With this unique schedule in seventh grade, my schedule in eighth grade was even more hectic. With no one else at my math level, I was tutored every morning by my high school principal during first period. This was just another "obstacle" I had to deal with in school concerning my education in math, since I was moving at a faster pace than my peers in this area academically. Although these experiences proved to be challenging, and I was tempted not to take them on, I am now glad I chose to tackle such hardships.

Fortunately, living in Chicago, I had many high schools from which to choose. By the middle of eighth grade, I had narrowed my selection to four Catholic schools. The night before the entrance exam, I made the decision to attend Regina Dominican High School, an all-girl school in the suburb of Wilmette. I guess my reasons for selecting Regina were that the girls there really took pride in their academic abilities and the school was well known for its accomplishments in the fields of mathematics and science, including placing first in the state for Worldwide Youth in Science and Engineering (WYSE). The girls there were not intimidated by boys and were free to express themselves. If anything, it is considered "cool" to stand out in mathematics and science. There is also a sense of strength from the girls in that they believe they can be the best at math and science even in the presence of males. The pride and confidence, which the girls displayed, only helped to promote my interest in science and math. In order to become more acquainted with the field of mathematics, we studied the writings of Sir Isaac Newton. While the reading was long and difficult, his discoveries inspired me to learn more about the profession of mathematics and really caused me to think about what formulas and theories were really saying in mathematics.

Once at Regina, I made a large circle of friends who focused on all areas of school life, but math and science remained my favorites. During my freshman year I was invited to join "Mathletes," the school math team. We practiced every Wednesday, which finally paid off at the regional meet. There I placed in the individual algebra competition, and our eight-person team placed in all areas. As a sophomore I continued to participate on the math team. Now, as a junior, I hope to lead the team to greater success and try to get more people involved. Currently, the math team does not receive a lot of recognition. I hope to change this by gaining support and having the team become a leading club at Regina.

Looking back on my experiences in the areas of mathematics and science, I realize it is my parents who have helped me succeed. Watching them go through college, I learned that sometimes you do have to struggle to make it through school, but your goals are always achievable. I also learned that you could use these fields of learning as areas of individual uniqueness (i.e., being the only seventh grader in a class of eighth graders). During these times, I was also learning more about my Native American culture. I learned that while rarely do Native Americans make it past high school (my family included), once given the chance, it is possible to excel at any level. Now, as a young, Native American women, I know it is an honor to be given the chance to learn at a higher level. Also, I know I can succeed from realizing what other women and Native Americans have accomplished. Most people are given the chance to succeed, but it is how one utilizes this opportunity that makes all the difference.

Looking back on all that I have done, I realize the smallest accomplishment is still something to celebrate. As a young woman, I see how hard it is for women to break into male-dominated areas. Attending an all-girl school, I still see the stereotypes from male schools concerning girls' abilities in math and science. Throughout the ages, women have proven to be strong when faced with such prejudices.

If I could give just one piece of advice to all young women and girls, it would be to take your talents in math and science and make them unique. Take pride in what you know and don't back down when questioned about your abilities. Uniqueness comes in all forms, mine just happens to be in mathematics and science. If at any time girls or young women are struggling to decide if science/math/technology should be their profession, I just hope that they remember they could be breaking into a profession that many women do not usually enter. The areas of mathematics, science, and technology still hold stereotypes that favor men. The only way to break such stereotypes is to prove people wrong, which any woman is capable of doing. Just as I was first unsure of this interest, I soon learned the support that women have for one another. Success will always come if you simply try.

ELINA
ONITSKANSKY

E lina Onitskansky was born in Odessa, Ukraine, May 14, 1984, to Alla and Michael Onitskansky. When Elina was six, her family and she immigrated to Cleveland, Ohio. Early on, Elina excelled in math and science. Her love for science led her to join Hathaway Brown's Research Seminar program. At the same time, Elina pursues many other activities. She is Junior Volunteer Coordinator at an area nursing home, where she has volunteered since fourth grade. She also participates in many clubs including the World Affairs Club of which she is vice president, the Foreign Language Club, the Environmental Club for which she is secretary, Drama Club, Mao Alpha Theta (math club), and yearbook staff. She is the school newspaper's Current Events Editor, a council member for the Young Activists for a Multicultural Community, and a member of TEAMS (a science and engineering competition). Elina's responsibility and determination to succeed and her thirst for knowledge best characterize her.

MICROELECTROCHEMICAL SENSOR

My project is a microelectrochemical sensor and plating system to detect and remove cadmium, copper, lead, nickel, iron, and zinc from water. Basically, a microelectrochemical sensor is a sensor that is about .75 by .75 centimeters. It has a working electrode and a reference electrode, which are like the cathode and the anode of a battery. A voltage can be applied to them to produce a current. A lot of my project deals with testing for the voltage versus current relationship at different concentrations of my metals. The concentrations that I am dealing with are very small—they are in parts per million. The reason for such small concentrations is that the metals are toxic even in very small quantities. Another part of my project encompassed the effect that the metals had on each other during testing. This is called interference. Finally, the plating system looks like my microsensor. It functions by causing the metals to bond with it chemically after a voltage is applied, and thereby removes the metals from the water. This process is similar to the way you can copper coat a nail.

My project is rather complex, and I obviously did not simply think it up. In fact, I started my research project in an unusual manner. In ninth grade I started Hathaway Brown School. When I was filling out what classes I wanted to take, a class under science caught my eye. It was labeled "Research Seminar." I asked the upper-school director what it was. As this was the start of the program, she vaguely explained that it would involve lab projects in science. This sounded interesting to me since I had always liked science, so I signed up for the course. Science has always appealed to me because it is at the same time an explanation and a puzzle. On one hand, science helps us to understand the world around us. Yet, at the same time, the study of science makes us aware of how much we don't know. Because of the appeal that science held for me, I read a lot of books and articles on the subject. The articles that most interested me were on Marie Curie, whose ability to fit science experiments into her life is mind-boggling. I also gained interest from newspaper articles that explained things being discovered now. Once I started the class, Mrs. Hunt, the advisor for Research Seminar, explained that each of us would get to work at an area lab, a *real* lab! Now, I was really excited. This wasn't going to be some done-over-and-over-again science project, it was going to be something new. When Mrs. Hunt asked me what I wanted to do, the creation of microsensors with Dr. C. C. Liu interested me. I have been working with Dr. Liu ever since. I am now a junior, which means that I have been working at the lab for over two years.

When I went to meet Dr. Liu, I expected to do some small steps in one of his projects. Instead, he asked me what I wanted to do for *my* project. I was really excited and decided that I would do something to aid the environment and people. So, I spent some time on the Internet researching different problems. I had already been exposed to some of the problems caused by lead poisoning, yet I was unaware of how many other metals there are that are just as harmful. My research led me to conclude that cadmium, copper, lead, nickel, iron, and zinc were some of the most problematic metals for the environment and for human health. Their problem is twofold. Not only are they toxic in small quantities, but they are also used in a multitude of ways. So, in an attempt to help solve this problem, I began working on a microelectrochemical sensor and plating system to detect and remove these elements. Little did I know how hard this process would be.

The first summer was the worst—everything went wrong. I went to the lab two full days a week that summer, and I can't say that anything at all got accomplished. I remember one day that I just kept testing and results kept coming back blank. It was depressing. However, Dr. Liu, Mrs. Hunt, and my parents continually encouraged me. Most of all, I knew that I couldn't just give up. I don't even think that it was a conscious choice to continue even when I felt that I would never progress. I simply didn't let myself imagine that I could just quit. I wasn't a quitter. So I kept working and things got better. Everything just began to fall into place. All of a sudden, I began to make progress. You cannot imagine what it felt like to succeed after so much failure. I think that made the success sweeter, when I knew that I had earned it with hard work and determination. I should mention that there are still days when I go down to the lab and return depressed and exhausted, but that's the nature of research. Nothing ever simply goes smoothly. You have to work for it. For every time that I succeeded, I failed twice. The important thing is that I didn't give up, I didn't say, "It's impossible."

I think the experience of overcoming failure was rewarding in itself. It taught me that if I were determined to do something, it would happen, no matter how unlikely it might seem at some points. I also learned to be patient. When you do high school labs, you have a time frame, and everything goes well and according to schedule. You get your results and everything is great. Real lab work is not like that. In *Jurassic Park,* one of the scientists says, "If it can go wrong, it will go wrong." Sometimes research is like that. The important thing is to put up with the hard times and keep working. It's the only way to succeed. I learned to throw away my timetables and just work. Yet, while both the ability to overcome failure and the ability to maintain patience are valuable, the experience I gained from creating is invaluable.

I learned so much about problem solving in the lab. At first, when I would go down to the lab and anything went wrong, I would have to ask for someone's help. It didn't matter how small the problem; I was unsure how to deal with it. I am proud to say that this last summer, I must have worked at the lab for about twenty hours a week, every week, and I only asked for help once, and it was because of faulty machinery. It was such a great feeling to look back and see how far I had come. I also had to approach many problems creatively. No one had ever done a microsensor to detect the metals I am detecting. Therefore, the problems that I ran into were often unique. I had to step back and just try a multitude of things to establish what the problem was, and only then could I begin to try and solve it. One example of this was the detection of zinc. When I started to detect zinc, it simply wouldn't work. So, I tried testing an unreasonably high concentration of zinc. When that didn't work, I knew there was something about zinc that was causing my sensor to be ineffective. To learn more, I read about zinc and its properties and talked with a few professors. The combination convinced me that zinc was too active for the working electrode I was using and that I would have to add another working electrode. In this case, I had no precedent to work with on what to do. I just had to try out different possibilities. At first, nothing worked, but through educated trial and error I was able to hit on the problem.

I can't say that now it is all smooth sailing. I still run into glitches, even though I am only a few months from the completion of my project. I have at this point perfected a design from a selection of ten different design types. I have used that design to test for each metal separately, as well as in combination with each other. Now I am putting the finishing touches on my invention. At completion, the microsensor will detect metals that cause cancer, child poisoning, and harm to fish and other animals. It will also save thousands of dollars because it is cost efficient. Right now I am in the process of putting the finishing touches on the sensor, and I am also starting the plating system. Now, when I encounter problems, I breathe deeply, go home, come back the next day, and try again.

I have received a patent for the microsensor and that was amazing. It made me step back and realize that everything I had worked and continued to work for is meaningful. I would like to thank everyone who helped me so much in pursuing the creation of this microsensor. My pursuit of this project has mostly been well received. People who hear of my project are usually amazed and supportive. Yet, there are those who have told me that this type of work was not meant for high school students, or that I had done everything incorrectly, or that it is not a good project. I try to ignore them and focus on the positive responses I have received. I wish good luck to anyone who wants to invent something. Things will be hard at times, I guarantee it. But if you stick with it, you're bound to succeed. I know I did.

CALLIE & ASHLI PFEIFFER | MAGGIE & SABRINA KELLEY

*C*allie and Ashli Pfeiffer are sisters. Callie was born October 18, 1985, and Ashli was born May 14, 1987. They live in Hamel, Minnesota, and have attended Orono Public School since the first grade and kindergarten. Life for them includes caring for the many animals on their property, reading, cooking (sometimes in roller blades), playing basketball and soccer, being with friends, and creating films. Callie likes to repair things like VCRs, computers, and stereos and has been interested in video cameras since the age of ten. Ashli is a prolific reader, outstanding student, and storywriter. Although she has juvenile rheumatoid arthritis, her knack for writing gives an amazing addition to the team.

Maggie and Sabrina Kelley are twin sisters who were born November 18, 1984. From kindergarten to sixth grade they attended Orono Public School, then went to a private middle school until the eighth grade, and are now back attending Orono Public School. They have lived in Orono, Minnesota, their entire lives. Maggie has always been fascinated by sound and audio technology and spends her free time working on the audio details that no one else would notice. Sabrina enjoys photography, painting, leadership, snowboarding, and writing.

YOUNG FILMMAKERS

We met in 1995 when we became next-door neighbors. Our talent and love for making movies became noticeable when we discovered we were spending most of our time with the video camera. One day, a friend told us about the National Children's Film Festival (NCFF) and teased us when we wanted to enter. "You can't do that, you're just girls!" So, of course, this only made us want to do it more!

We got together and started brainstorming for a story idea. Between our two families we have a lot of animals, which we wanted to use in the movie. So we wrote a story about a gang of ducks that kidnap a puppy out of revenge against dogs, and all the farm animals blame the local fox because of his bad reputation. Basically, the story is about prejudice.

We filmed after school and on weekends for about six weeks. It was difficult to film this movie because none of the animals were trained, and they wouldn't do what we told them to do. For instance, the puppy was supposed to go off on a journey with the bad ducks, but the ducks were afraid of the puppy, so we couldn't get them in many shots together. We had to splice them together using a computer. It took a lot of organizing and planning to get all the scenes completed in time for the NCFF deadline.

We had never done any editing before, but we were confident that we could learn. We bought an inexpensive editing software program called Avid Cinema, but our computer didn't have enough memory to install the program. We had to go to Callie and Ashli's uncle's house in Chicago over spring break to use his computer to try and get the editing done in four days. When we arrived in Chicago, we worked about fifteen hours each day for the four days and got the film done in time to enter it in the NCFF. The title of our movie is *Benny*.

In August, we heard that we had won first place in the middle school category. It was the most exciting day of our lives. We were jumping up and down, screaming at the top of our lungs. We won $2,000 for the movie, and it was acquired by HBO Family Channel to be shown on a program they air called *30 by 30 Kids Flicks*. We got lots of publicity like *Good Morning America*, *USA Today*, the *Ladies Home Journal*, *TIME for Kids*, the *Wall Street Journal*, and local newspapers.

After the 1999 movie *Benny* was finished, we immediately started writing another story for a movie. This one was a lot more complicated and involved human actors, not animals. By this time we had a new camera and our own editing computer. The software we wanted was complicated, but after researching several options, it was the only one we thought would meet our needs for the new movie and future movies.

We were talking to a producer from New York, telling him that we were going to get Adobe Premiere software and he said, "That is way over your heads. Get something simple. I have been making movies for twenty years and Adobe Premiere is over my head." We didn't want to hurt his feelings, but we had already tested it on the manufacturer's Web site, and we thought it was a piece of cake. Callie said to him, "It might be over your head, but it is not over ours."

We timed our second movie over about a six-month period. It took a huge amount of planning and some serious head butting on the team, but we got it done. The editing took six more weeks. We learned a lot about computers on this movie because the computer kept messing up and we had to figure out how to fix it. We got it done in time to enter it in the 2000 NCFF.

We heard in early September 2000 that we had won the Creative Excellence Award in the middle school category for this movie called *Pushing Back the Limits*. It is about a young girl from Germany in the late 1800s and how many limits she placed on herself because she was "a girl." We compared the story to our own lives now, showing how far girls have come because of people fighting for women's rights.

We are currently working on a movie specifically for HBO Family Channel. We were hired to write and make a movie, and we were chosen by HBO as one of the top ten kid filmmakers in the country.

ASHLEE
RIDDLE

orn June 13, 1983, in Nashville, Tennessee, Ashlee and her parents soon moved to Baltimore, Maryland. She lived in Maryland for twelve years, attending Garrison Forest School, Roland Park Country School, and Notre Dame Preparatory. When she was twelve, her parents divorced, and she moved to Elgin, Illinois, with her mother, two younger sisters, and younger brother. There she attended the Illinois Mathematics and Science Academy in Aurora, Illinois, where she pursued her interests in science through the Academy's Mentorship program. She was captain of the girls' varsity swim team, coeditor of Real Science CD-ROM *magazine, a National History Day participant, and a member of the varsity softball team. She plays the piano and bass guitar. Her strongest role model is her mother, Lorelei Ann Keltner, because of her dedication to her family, her ambition, and her kindness toward others.*

RAPID PROTOTYPING

I have spent the past three years working in the Mechanical Engineering Department at the University of Illinois at Chicago one day a week and throughout the summer. My research has focused on materials processing, specifically rapid prototyping (RP) techniques and binder burnout (BBO) methods. RP is a system created to fabricate solid three-dimensional models from computer data, from bottom to top, one layer at a time. BBO is a process in which the weak materials are removed from the RP model to provide maximum strength. When attempting to create porous structures, we ran into a problem because the RP machine is only intended to create solid models. For the first two years of my research, I focused on finding a way to fabricate porous structures using RP equipment.

The applications for this research range greatly, from space travel to submarine parts to medical miracles. NASA is interested in this technology for its upcoming shuttle launch to Mars. If shuttles were to have RP machines onboard with part designs already stored in the computer, astronauts could simply "print out" a replacement part if needed. This would save money, time, and space. The United States Navy uses RP-created parts in submarine propellers because of their strength and structural properties. Our lab is also working on a project using MRI data to create replacement bones for shattered bones that are unable to heal, as an alternative solution to amputation or false limbs. These RP-fabricated bones are made out of material similar to bone and are porous in order to allow the surrounding tissue to grow into the replacement and let it naturally fit into place. This replacement bone could easily be redesigned to accommodate a patient's growth over the years by simply taking an MRI of the opposite leg, arm, hip, or other such parts and creating a new bone to meet the new dimensions.

The main focus of this research was to learn how to generate controlled porous structures with specific applications, and to manufacture ceramic filter elements for high-temperature environments. When we began our research, there was no existing technology capable of generating porous models. However, we combined several modeling programs and discovered how to design a structure that would meet the desired performance specifications. We experimented with Rinoceros Beta (RB) and Stratasys Quick Slice (QS) programs. RB is a program designed to create three-dimensional blueprints. Then, using the QS program we translate these blueprints into files that the RP machine can read. With an understanding of the RB and QS programs, we could command the machine to ignore the default settings. This led us to the development of various numerical mesh generation configurations. We could then fabricate various porous structures to determine pore architecture and permeability to fluid flow.

Currently, I am involved in the development of new BBO methods for ceramics using plasma gases. Our research from the past two years taught us how to manipulate the software in order to create the desired outcome. Now that we can create more advanced structures, we are attempting to create stronger structures by using ceramic filaments in place of plastic filaments. The RP machine was not produced to use ceramic filaments, however, so wax needs to be added to the filament in order for it to flow smoothly through the machine and create a finished model. Once the structure is completed, the wax needs to be removed. This year we are testing a new theoretical method of removing the wax binder.

Traditionally, BBO involves heating a structure in an oven-like setting until the wax is removed. We are using plasma gases to attempt to remove the wax binder faster and with less damage to the original structure. This method is theoretically estimated to work two hundred times faster than the oven method. It will also create a smoother finish on the final product because this method removes the binder from the outside in, instead of from the inside out. This method will prevent excess binder and water caught within the structure from forming bubbles and blemishes on the finished surfaces.

On TV and in movies you see futuristic scenarios where characters go to their computer and a football pops out of the printer or scuba gear appears in the living room after clicking on the icon from a sporting gear Web page. This project proves that the idea is not as futuristic as you may think.

ANADELIZ SANCHEZ
ROMAN

*A*nadeliz Sanchez Roman was born May 26, 1982. Her first school years meant very much to her because she loved her teachers, helped classmates, and participated in science fairs. At this stage of her life, it made her happy and satisfied to help others. For example, she has served as a mentor for a girl with both physical and mental disabilities, an experience in which she learned to value her strengths. She has participated in various science and math competitions and has won prizes and recognition for her accomplishments.

SUCCESS IN SCIENCE FAIRS

I had the opportunity to participate in science and biology workshops with projects such as *Parents Academic Preparation vs. The Academic Preparation of Their Children* and *The Academic Preparation of The Elder and Their Economic Stability.* These enabled me to learn skills that helped later in my own investigations.

With the investigation project the *Math and Science Campus and The Student Gender*, I participated in the Math and Science Congress sponsored by the University of Puerto Rico. I also had the opportunity to be part of the Puerto Rico delegation and participate in the National Symposium of Science and Humanities celebrated in New Mexico, which was a gratifying experience because I was able to participate in different project expositions at a national level. I was given an award by the Government Ethics Office of Puerto Rico in March 1998 for my essay entitled "The New Ethnic Generation."

During the summer of that same year, I was invited to participate in a summer camp sponsored by the University of Puerto Rico and the teachers' association of science, where I was exposed to all of the science fields. The camp was called "Nurturing Future Scientific Research Academy for Secondary School Students." This experience helped me reassure myself that investigative work is what I want to do. I've had to struggle very much but results are satisfying. The help from my teachers and family has been an essential factor in reaching my goals. Another one of them is belonging to a competitive Puerto Rican team in the international fair. This opportunity was given to me after participating in the 1999 science fair.

The *Selection of Vocational Careers and Students Gender* was one of the greatest goals I reached. Recently I participated in the District Fair of San Sebastian with my project and won first place in science classification of the conduct, and it also received the highest recognition among all of the projects that were presented at this fair. I participated in the Regional Fair of Mayaguez with my project and obtained first place in science classification of the conduct again. This project came about through the realization that life is impacted by our choices and decisions. The techniques of investigation used in this research were the distribution of 144 questionnaires, to students of different years of study at the University of Puerto Rico. Fifty percent of those interviewed were females and 50 percent were males. The factors investigated within this study included education of parents, place of the study center, part- or full-time jobs, parental income, and job opportunities. The data revealed that a direct relationship exists between the factors presented in this research and the selection of the academic careers of the college students.

According to the results, there are more females influenced by the factors than males. All of these factors together are very important in the life of each individual person at the time he or she chooses an academic career.

One of the biggest obstacles in my investigation projects has been sample identification, but I am very persistent and I don't quit until I finish something and make it a reality. This quality has been a factor that has determined all my accomplished goals. If you say you can do something, you can and I've always said I can.

AMY BETH
SALTZMAN

*A*my Beth Saltzman's premature entrance into this world has shaped her future endeavors. Born April 14, 1983, Amy was two months early and only weighed three pounds, fourteen ounces. Two years later, her parents, Shelly and Mark, had a second child, Andrew, yet again eight weeks early. Their premature births have led Amy to activities and future plans in neonatology. The Saltzmans' have grown up in Cleveland, Ohio, and Amy has attended Hathaway Brown School since kindergarten. The independent school has helped shape Amy's interests and ambitions. Science has always been Amy's passion, from her primary school inventions to her current genetics research. She integrates science and medicine into her everyday life, conducting research at Case Western Reserve University and volunteering in the Neonatal Intensive Care Unit at University Hospitals of Cleveland. Additionally, projects involving community service and fundraising have enabled Amy to support research, as well as other local and international causes.

SPINAL MUSCULAR ATROPHY RESEARCH

Almost four years ago, my infant friend, Preston Fisher, was diagnosed with Spinal Muscular Atrophy (SMA) at the age of seven months. SMA is a genetic neuromuscular disease that is the leading cause of death in children under the age of two. Although many have never heard of this fatal disease, one in forty people is a carrier. A lack of the survival motor neuron protein (SMN) causes a person's muscles to atrophy and all muscle function to deteriorate, eventually causing heart and lung failure.

Immediately after I found out about Preston's diagnosis, I wanted to find a way to help search for a cure for the disease. I began to focus on monetary aid, and cochaired a fundraiser at my school to raise money for the Preston Fund for SMA Research at Ohio State University. Along with a friend, Emily McGinty, I organized an entire day dedicated to Preston. Events included a bake sale, a dress-down day, a raffle, a walkathon (walkers receive pledges to walk a certain number of laps), general donations, and a speech by Dr. Arthur Burghes of Ohio State University. The Hathaway Brown community pulled together in a way that it never had before to support a cause that touched each of us. It seemed as if each member of the school community cared personally about finding a cure for SMA. The school raised almost five thousand dollars for SMA research.

Although I had helped monetarily, I wanted to find a more hands-on, direct approach to assist in finding a cure for SMA. It took me a very long time to find the opportunity that I wanted, and I turned down many others in the process. Heart valve labs, breast cancer researchers, and even NASA employees had offered to grant me the chance to take part in preeminent research, but I insisted on waiting to participate in SMA research. After quite some time, I spoke to Dr. Burghes, an SMA investigator at Ohio State University, and inquired about the SMA research opportunities in Cleveland. Although none existed, he suggested that I look for related research in my area. I talked to Dr. Huntington Willard, head of the Genetics Department at Case Western Reserve University, and he directed me to Dr. A. Gregory Matera, a professor in his department. Greg's lab studies a protein called p-80 coilin and the coiled body, a nuclear organelle in which high concentrations of that protein exist. SMN, the protein which is missing in SMA patients, and p-80 coilin have been shown to interact. Therefore, by studying coilin and coiled bodies I would be participating in the quest for a cure for SMA! I considered Preston's everlasting fight to overcome the struggle of SMA, and I decided that I would invest my time and effort into coilin research.

Venturing into the world of scientific research is a big step for any high school student. A fifteen-year-old's peers are generally fifteen-year-olds, so a sudden jump to work with twenty-five-year-olds is both challenging and enticing. When I first met my lab buddies, I was a little nervous. I worried that they might think of me as immature, inexperienced, and incapable. However, once I met them, not only did they seem incredibly friendly and willing to help me get used to the lab, but they treated me as an equal and as a peer, making my time in the lab not only a great learning experience, but also a blast! Each of them added something to my lab experience. Michael, my first mentor, organizes everything to perfection and made my entrance into the lab a breeze. Karen, my second mentor, really knows how to relate to everyone and is an incredible teacher with a lot of patience. Greg always enters intensely, ready to talk about anything, from research to mountain climbing. Mark and Jen add humor to the lab, making everyone burst into giggles at least once an hour. Christy always has some new random fact to announce, and Li-Ming never comes in in the morning without a cheery hello. The social aspect of the lab helped me immensely in learning how to function in an environment very different from school or home. In the end, the relationships I formed at the lab became as important to me as the research I completed.

Laboratory procedures can seem quite overwhelming at first, but I owe a lot of my background to my freshman year research biology class. Dr. Lorelei Davis, a teacher with whom I first worked my eighth grade year, became my mentor in ninth grade. She advised me on everything from friendships to lab opportunities. Additionally, along with two seniors completing a school project in which they organized a program for upper-school students to learn how to use advanced science technology, she helped me learn how to run an agarose gel, transform DNA into bacteria, and use a pipette. Those basic skills made learning how to do polymerese chain reactions (PCR), gel electrophoresis, restriction digests, mini-preps, DNA transformations, tissue cultures, 5' rapid amplification of cDNA ends (RACE), and T-A cloning much easier, because I had some experience using laboratory tools and protocols. This is not to say that I did not have difficulties at times learning new concepts or procedures. Just like many other new researchers, I have dropped gels, spilled solutions, thrown out tubes containing important DNA, and left enzymes on the bench at room temperature. However, I came through all of these bloopers, and I have become a more accomplished scientist because of them.

Although Dr. Davis was my first mentor, I have had others. Mrs. Patty Hunt, my second backbone in terms of science research, was my primary source of encouragement when times got tough. When you involve yourself in this type of intense activity, you must find a mentor to help you deal with your frustrations and celebrate you victories. Mrs. Hunt stayed at school until nine o'clock some nights, waiting for me to finish my presentations at the last minute to enter into a symposium, and she was the first to see my smile as I walked down from the stage after receiving a scholarship at Intel Science and Engineering Fair.

Practice reading professional scientific abstracts and articles from magazines such as *Science, Science News,* and *Scientific American* has helped me grasp some of the complicated terminology and protocols involved in genetics research. Additionally, I have learned a lot about the scientific method and designing a controlled experiment by looking at articles both related and completely unrelated to my own research. Besides, some of the information that I learned while reading the magazines is so interesting! I have read about topics from possible diabetes cures to a gene that has been cloned into a monkey.

Throughout my involvement in SMA research, I have found inspiration in Preston. The image of his adorable smile and the sound of his sweet voice motivate me, for I know that there are hundreds of other children around the world struggling with the same disease. At times when I have considered not entering a research symposium because I have had a lot of work to do, or on those days when I have been incredibly tired and not willing to focus intensely for hours, I consider my purpose for the research and renew my strength to continue my own battle against SMA. The thought of Preston has helped to get me to where I am today, but additionally, my history at Hathaway Brown has aided me in reaching my goals. Being an all-girl school, Hathaway Brown has instilled a sense of ambition and self-confidence in me. I feel that I have an obligation to complete anything that I begin. I exert all of my effort into achieving any goal and always try to execute every task to the best of my ability. I sometimes wonder whether I would be different if I had grown up without Hathaway Brown. I cannot answer that question for sure, but I do know that the principles behind Hathaway Brown have become a part of me, and I can consider the school almost a third parent, helping to raise me with confidence, determination, persistence, and values.

So far, at three and a half, Preston has lived almost two years longer than expected and is doing very well; however, there is still no cure for SMA. My coilin research has recently begun to connect more closely to SMA because I have worked with mice lacking both the coilin gene and the SMN gene, yet I am still a long way from finding a solution to the elimination of Preston's ailments. I continue to work in the Matera lab, searching for the function of the coilin protein, and I have accomplished a lot since I started. Last year I determined the amino acid sequence of p-80 coilin in the rat. Scientists have been trying to find the amino acid sequence of coilin in various species. The alignment of those sequences warrants the identification of conserved regions of the sequence among the difference species. Those conserved regions, having been important enough to the coilin protein to stay intact throughout evolution, are most likely important to the coilin protein's function. I was a coauthor of the rat coilin sequence entry in the Genbank on-line database last spring. Additionally, I have traveled to Columbus, Ohio; Toledo, Ohio; and Detroit, Michigan, to share my findings. Last May, I was one of two students to move on from the Buckeye Science and Engineering Fair and travel to Michigan for the Intel International Science and Engineering Fair. Over two thousand students from forty countries displayed their research discoveries and shared their stories. I had the unique opportunity to meet many unbelievable young researchers, converse one-on-one with Ph.D.s from around the world, and even talk to a panel of eight Nobel laureates. Additionally, I was awarded fourth place in the biochemistry category, as well as a substantial scholarship to Lehigh University. The event was a once-in-a-lifetime experience, and my fervor for scientific research was enlivened by the week I spent in Detroit.

If I could give you one suggestion, it would not be to study p-80 coilin. It would not be to search for a cure for SMA. It would not even be to involve yourself in scientific research. Rather, I am telling you to find a passion and exert every bit of yourself in trying to fulfill your goals centered around that passion. Nothing can be as fulfilling as striving to achieve a goal that will help someone, something, or even yourself grow, change, and prosper. People are always looking too far into the future for meaning in life. They forget to step back and realize that anything can be accomplished in the present. If you set your mind to achieve your goals and put forth your entire self for the sake of your passions, you can overcome all challenges.

KYRA
SEDRANSK

*K*yra Sedransk was born August 29, 1985, to Joseph and Nell Sedransk. She has a brother, Eli, who is three years younger. Before moving to Shaker Heights, Ohio, where she currently resides, Kyra lived in many other places. After having lived in Connecticut, New York, and Iowa, Kyra moved with her family to Washington, D.C., where she attended the French International School. Before leaving three years later to move to Albany, New York, she had become fluent in French. In 1995 she moved again, to Shaker Heights, a suburb of Cleveland. At the start of 1996, Kyra transferred to Hathaway Brown School. During her sixth- and seventh-grade years, she was a vigorous participant in the schools' science fair and attended regional and state fairs. In eighth grade she began her work with Dr. K. Jane Grande-Allen at the Cleveland Clinic Foundation's Department of Biomedical Engineering. Her work with Dr. Grande-Allen has proved to be very successful and enjoyable.

MITRAL VALVE BIOMECHANICS

It was really scary the first time I went with our school's research program coordinator, Mrs. Patricia Hunt, to meet Dr. Grande-Allen. I was aware of the research I would be conducting, but I had no idea what I was in for. The first day we went to her lab, I was mortified to learn that we would actually dissect a pig heart so that she could show me what I was to study. I asked to be excused to go to the bathroom when she brought out the heart from its plastic sack. Now, I am really surprised I had the courage to return. After sticking my fingers into the heart and cutting it, *my* heart pounded. Even after leaving I never told anyone how my stomach had churned. Now, after having cut open about fifty pig hearts, I have no problem going home to a pot roast dinner. But, for the first few weeks, I never ate dinner after returning from the lab.

At first the lab was a little boring because I had to practice dissection techniques. I never realized that preparation was such detailed work. Famous scientists never talked about this part of the work in the biographies I read about them. And let me tell you, I screwed up more times than I can remember. Once I cut off the wrong part of the heart and threw it away. Of course I did not realize what I had done, so I continued to follow the procedure. When I failed to reach what I was looking for, I realized that what I needed was in the waste bin. I was able to rescue it before anyone knew, so I continued along as if nothing had happened. It took several weeks for me to get to the point where I could do the preparation skillfully enough to be ready for testing.

The purpose of my research was to test the strength of chordae, structures found in the mitral valve that aid in the sealing of the valve as it opens and closes to allow blood to flow through or not to flow through, respectively. It not only took me several weeks to master the technique of preparing the specimen, but it took time to understand the purpose of my research, too. As time passed, I became quite proficient. To test the specimen I had to learn a lot about special equipment that aided me in this process. I had to learn how to use some very specialized equipment, and I had to know how it worked as well. At first Dr. Grande-Allen and I spent a lot of time working together to test a specimen. Once I was competent with the procedure and the computer program, I worked on my own most of the time.

My project started off running in October and did not slow down until the following May. I worked diligently, hoping that I would be able to discover something very interesting and new about mitral valve biomechanics. I presented my research at several science fairs over the course of the year. The experience at regional and state fairs taught me a lot about the skills required in the presentation of scientific research. It also forced me to learn in even greater depth so that I could actually inform the judges about my exciting results. The scientific standards of the laboratory also forced me to take the time to analyze the data from many different points of view. I was very happy with my accomplishments.

When I started my freshmen year of high school, I decided to take a pause in my research to ensure that I could manage the work of high school. The year got off to a great start, and I discovered I had a real interest in politics and history, two subjects I had never really thought about. I participated in activities associated with the World Affairs Club at my school. Not wanting to leave my research behind, I decided to enter it into several competitions I had not been eligible for as a middle schooler. To prepare for these competitions, I worked with my mom to learn a lot about statistics to analyze my data in greater depth. The analyses did not take extremely long to do, but it took me a long time to learn about analysis and how it works. What I gained from learning about statistical analysis continues to help me with my research. I also mastered Corel Draw so that I could design the four-by-eight foot poster for the competitions. The competitions that I entered this year involved multiple-day meetings and podium presentations. Over the course of my freshman year, I made many presentations. From state competitions I was selected to attend multiple national and international competitions. At the larger competitions, I have had the opportunity to share my work with esteemed scientists, Nobel Prize winners, and government officials including David Satcher, the United States Surgeon General in the Clinton administration. The experience of teaching such important people about the research that I performed is one of the reasons I love to participate in these competitions. At these competitions I also met and made friends with other students from all over the world; some of us continue to correspond using e-mail. These incredible opportunities would never have been open to me without my diligence and hard work over two years.

Recently, I have resumed my research and am working on a paper for a technical journal. Reaching this point was a struggle. In December 1999, my grandmother passed away. We had never lived close by, but she had always been an inspiration to me. She worked very hard and was internationally recognized for her work in the study of African women and their literature. Though we are passionate about different things, I had always looked up to her as promoting the achievements of women. The intensity of her work and the reason she did it were the same as mine. We both love what we do. Her death inspired me to pursue my love for my research, to work hard at it, and to be recognized.

JENNIFER
SEILER

*J*ennifer was born May 5, 1983, in Washington, D.C. She is the daughter of
Steven Seiler, a plasma physician and senior scientist at Alme and Associates,
and Gretchen Seiler, Director of Executive Office Affairs at the American Association for the Advancement of Science (AAAS). At four years of age, Jennifer moved
to northern Virginia where she took up soccer, figure skating, the saxophone, piano,
and horseback riding. She was the president of the computer club and a participant
in Inventions and Innovations in elementary school. When she entered high
school, she joined her school math team. Her main hobby, aside from research in the
sciences, is rock climbing. The influence of her mother has led her to have an acute
interest in the arts and literature. She has won numerous awards for her poetry and
has been published three times. She believes her place is in the physical sciences, and
her true passion is cosmology. She hopes to attend Princeton University.

ACOUSTIC THERMOMETRY OF SEA WATER

I feel lucky to have been born into one of the most exciting times in the history of humanity for the study of physics. I opened an e-mail just the other day to find the evidence of the Higgs boson was witnessed recently. One cannot imagine how excited I was to read this. I have been fortunate to have met Rocky Kolb and other influential scientists and to read the works of Steven Weinberg and Richard Feynman among others. Living in Washington, D.C. has afforded me the opportunity to attend conferences and lectures regularly and to interact with my peers each year when I attend the Intel Science and Technology finalists' project displays. Additionally, since the age of twelve, I have met and spoken with teenage girls who are succeeding and being recognized in science.

I am most interested in cosmology and astrophysics because these fields incorporate many of the various areas of science that pique my interest (i.e., particle physics, nuclear physics, astronomy, mathematics, computer science, fluid dynamics, thermodynamics, engineering, theoretical chemistry, and so on), and they are also extremely relevant to culture and the humanities in their effect on philosophy/religion, the perceptions of time, and the origin of the universe and its fate. Despite these fields' arguable lack of practical use, in the big picture, I find them to be some of the most relevant areas in the sciences. They answer questions of our origin, fate, and purpose to an even deeper degree than anthropology, paleontology, and microbiology.

The Acoustic Thermometry of Ocean Climates (ATOC) program being carried out by the National Oceanic and Atmospheric Administration (NOAA) this year inspired my Acoustic Thermometry of Sea Water project. The ATOC program is designed to measure global warming due to the greenhouse effect. A process known as sound fixing and ranging (SOFAR) is used to measure the average temperature of the ocean by sending and receiving sound pulses through the Pacific Ocean and measuring the speed at which the sound travels. By repeatedly launching signals, NOAA is capable of keeping a continuous tab on the ocean temperature, and therefore (so they say) on global warming.

My questions were: "How will the varying salinity in the ocean effect the ATOC's results?" "How does pressure effect the speed of sound in water?" and "Will the melting of icebergs, which will lower the salinity and increase the pressure for the ATOC system, cause discrepancies in the results? And if so, how much?" To answer these questions, I built a small apparatus that sent and received sound pulses and measured the time it took. The apparatus was built using a thirty-foot length of hose with two piezo-electric transducers from a Christmas card at either end. I constructed a pulse-emitter, which was hooked up to one of the transducers. The other transducer was used for detection. A universal counter system was then attached to the apparatus to time the speed of the pulses through the length of the hose. The hose was then filled with water of various temperatures and salinities and the speed calculated to determine the effects that temperature and salinity had on the speed of sound.

I soon discovered that I was calculating the speed of sound through the hose and not through the water. Water has a Poisson's ratio of one. This means the pressure applied in the axial direction of the object will be released the same in all dimensions; therefore, all the sound was being absorbed by the hose and traveled through it the rest of the distance. The only way to conduct the experiment accurately was to find some sort of container that has all dimensions similar in length. I calculated the most accurate possible length that would work for the purpose of this project would be about twenty feet. It would be impossible, with my resources, to do the project as planned; therefore, I decided to find the equations for the speed of sound in liquid and to calculate the data with variables of differing temperatures and salinities.

I discovered that the speed of sound increases on a curve with an increase in salinity. The speed of sound also increases with a rise in temperature. These results show that if global warming does effect the melting of icebergs, the outcome would be a decreased salinity of ocean water resulting in a lower speed of sound through it. This would somewhat counteract the effects of the increase in temperature on the speed of sound. Furthermore, the varying salinity in the ocean will affect results of the ATOC program, and continual checks on the different salinities of the test area should be conducted.

I selected this project because I found it both challenging and relevant not only to myself, but to my fellow students, and I wanted to be recognized for my scientific ability in such a way that someone other than a football player would make the morning announcements at school. Being only fourteen at the time, these were relevant reasons to me. I have always tended to try to make my assignments and education more valuable than it might be if I just conducted the assignments that were required by my teachers.

I continue to research areas of interest. This past summer, I conducted a seven-week research project at the National Superconducting Cyclotron Laboratory (NSCL) at Michigan State University as part of a program called the High School Honors Science Program (HSHSP) under the supervision of Dr. Gary Westfall. Approximately twenty-five high school students are selected from the United States and its territories to attend the program. Each student is assigned an independent research project in various subject areas. I selected a project in nuclear physics entitled "Longitudinal Flow in Au+Au Collisions from 20 to 60 AmeV." For this project I studied the nucleons after collisions at Fermi energies in a direction parallel to the incident beam.

I have faced very few challenges in my efforts to pursue physics. I can complain of little more than ridicule, which has been based more on my dedication than my gender or age. My parents have been encouraging, as have all of the scientists and professors whom I have had the privilege of meeting. I attend a school in the most diverse school district in the nation, and the only belief not tolerated in my environment is that of bigotry. The fact that I am currently the only girl in my computer systems college course and that I am one of few girls taking the higher level of AP physics has not discouraged me. While the males in these classes have never taken any offense to me as a female, the fact that I am usually the highest achiever in those classes often intimidates them.

I would encourage other girls not to be intimidated because you are unique or alone. If you know that physical differences are meaningless for skin color and origin, then you should know that it goes for gender as well. Be encouraged by your uniqueness and by the freshness of what you are doing. You should know that anyone trying to hold you back is probably not going anywhere themselves. Take full advantage of the resources available to you, and remember that no one person can truly hold you back from your interests except you.

JACKIE
SWANSON

*J*ackie Swanson was born January 21, 1987, in San Francisco, California. She lives with her mom in California, and the rest of her family lives in Las Vegas. She attends Davidson Middle School and doesn't have a favorite class because she enjoys everything about school. However, if she had to choose, it would be drama or art.

Some of her personality traits include perseverance, individuality, wit, vigor, and persistence, all of which make her a great inventor. She is also genuinely stubborn and will stick with something until there is no other way to make it any better.

GIRL TECH

I'm a thirteen-year-old inventor. My mom and I create toys for girls ages eight to fourteen, and they are nothing like Barbie. Not that Barbie is bad or anything, it's just that after girls turn about seven, they start to get tired of Barbie and look for something new. Unfortunately, there wasn't much of a market for girls after what I call the *A.B.* (After Barbie) Era. Girls had nowhere to go and nothing to do, and it was a problem. This is one of the reasons we started Girl tech.

When I was about eight, my mom and I had created our first toy, Yak-bak. It was the first toy out on the market that allowed children to record their voices and play them back to themselves at affordable prices. Anyway, I remember I was sitting in the living room doing my homework, when the commercial for Yak-bak came on television. I ran to get my mom; we were so happy to see a commercial for our product. However, when we had finished watching it, we weren't so happy anymore. The commercial was directed toward boys, while the girls were the props, cheerleaders, or victims, even though the toy was meant to be gender neutral. I turned around in my seat and asked my mom, "Why'd they make it for boys?"

"Good question," was her response, and that's when we decided to start Girl tech.

Ever since then, we have been going all around the world giving talks and influencing people to respect women and girls. I always go with my mom to give talks. I think this is one of the best things that this company has done for me. I'm not afraid at all to get up in front of large audiences and talk. One of the biggest audiences I talked in front of consisted of about 2,500 people. I was around eleven at that time, and I wasn't the least bit afraid since I had experience in front of large groups when I was little! Usually I end up talking the most, and I make the people laugh and loosen them up to make it fun. I love it!

While starting this business, there were many obstacles we had to overcome. Some where little things. For example, when we went to New York for Toy Fair, we had to decide whether we should go the Empire State Building or visit the art museum near Central Park. Some were big things like when Hasbro showed our toys at Toy Fair and marketed them in pink or when we went to Toy Fair for three years straight and were on the edge of failure and funding before we were saved by Radica. Most of these obstacles I didn't have to worry about too much, since my mom is so good at handling these kinds of things. I mainly had to worry about whether I wanted to go to the art museum, Empire State Building, or Central Park. Heh, heh.

I think my mom would be my biggest influence throughout all of this. She would be my biggest female role model. I don't know anyone else that could even come close. If I had a choice, I would do it all over again. It was so much fun, and we got to go to all these cool places like New York, Texas, China, and Ohio. I especially liked when we went to Florida to see Eileen Collins, the first female commander, launch into space. Afterward I even got to meet Hillary Clinton! It was so fun . . . I wish I could do it all again.

I gained so many things throughout this entire experience. I learned to overcome my fears and do my absolute best, despite what everyone else said. I learned to follow my gut instinct and always think of others when making a decision. I also came to realize that the best offer isn't always the right one. I improved my ability in knowing how to read people, and how to be polite and act nice to people even if they have bad teeth or are annoying and rude, so that we can get that deal to make a new toy. But mostly, I learned to love myself for what I had accomplished and to always follow my heart.

EVELINA ALICIA
TERAN

velina Alicia Teran was born in Tucuman, Argentina, July 31, 1984. She has one brother, Guillermo (thirteen), and one sister, Lucrecia (eleven). She grew up in a family with scientific and naturalist interests. Her mother, Marcela, is a botanist, and her father, Enrique, is a science education teacher. She loves animals and is devoted to the rehabilitation of injured wild birds.

Evelina attends the Colegio Pablo Apostol, Yerba Buena, Tucuman. Since her early school years she has taken part in science fairs with great enthusiasm. Regional and international precollege science and engineering fairs experiences lifted her spirit and strengthened her vocation. She founded and is president of the Donald Griffin Science Club, which encourages the formation of youth groups in research projects. Her main scientific interest is scorpions and their incidence in public health. She collaborates with hospitals, determining the scorpions that provoke accidents.

SCORPIONS: DANGEROUS CLONES

My concern about the increase in the number of scorpion sting accidents in towns of fourteen Argentine provinces led me to work out a model of research on the biology and epidemiology of the *Tityus trivittatus* scorpion.

Tityus trivittatus is a scorpion that represents a serious epidemiological problem in Argentina, determined by a series of biological characteristics: its anthropic habits, its parthenogenetic reproduction, its defensive behavior, and its neurotoxic venom. This scorpion belongs to the Buthidae family, and its area of geographic distribution also includes Paraguay and southern Brazil. These scorpions feed on crickets, cockroaches, and other insects during twilight and the nightime hours. The spread of the species is facilitated by means of transport. Due to the absence of males in numerous populations of this species and their rapid propagation, I gave these lines of descendents the name of "Dangerous Clones." These clones have conquered human dwellings and all types of house-like habitats; sometimes being conveyed along pipes even up to the seventh floor of a building.

In 1998, when I was thirteen, I came into contact with several specialists on scorpions in my country: Drs. Emilio Maury, Jose Corronca, and Alfredo Peretti. In 1999, at a postgraduate course on Dangerous Arachnids in Argentina, Dr. Corronca stated that my contribution was the most up-to-date for the country. My contributions to the progress of the scientific knowledge on scorpions are the use of electronic microphotography in the definition of the perceptual world of scorpions; the first photographic documentation, in a series, of the birth of the *Tityus trivittatus* scorpion; verification of complex nonreported behavior in scorpions; biogeographic characterization of the Northwestern Argentina species; communication of the epidemiologic situation of scorpionism; discussion on the parthenogenesis in *Tityus trivittatus*; and the invention of a device for extracting venom.

I wondered what structures allowed scorpions to occupy such unexpected spaces as a safe or a telephone box. To solve this problem I prepared some material to make a study of their structures by electron microscope. I was fascinated by the diversity and subtlety of sensory organs, which includes mechanoreceptors and chemoreceptors. A series of photos of their sensory pegs, forms in the teeth of the pectines (ventral structures exclusive to scorpions), allowed me to discover their secretory function, when only the sensorial function had been described. It is still to be discovered whether these secretions allow the animal to fasten itself to the substrate, or to be at the service of intraspecific communication (between females naturally).

All scorpions are viviparous (bear live young). Their birth behavior and the transport of the offspring by the mother are fascinating aspects of their biology. While the mother adopts the birth basket position, up to eighteen offspring are born which climb her body. Their transport on the back of the female supplies the offspring with protection and a suitable microenvironment in regards to humidity, shade, and temperature. Under conditions of stress, there is cannibalism of the mother toward her offspring.

I did not expect to report the behavior of a female who eliminated one young immature offspring with a precise blow from her sting that threw the offspring 13 cm away. I also observed a cooperative mother-offspring relationship sharing captured prey with an already independent offspring. These observations encourage further research into the functional aspects of scorpion behavior.

Concerned about integrating the conservation of biodiversity and epidemiological context of the ecoregions, I made an assessment of bioindicator species in different localities and communities representative of the cultural and natural diversity of Tucuman. Contrary to what Maury and other scientists supposed, that only *Tityus trivittatus* caused accidents, my data suggests that other species cause them too. This is partly due to the fact that the rural and Indian dwellings of the local communities offer favorable microenvironments (stone and wood). I was able to verify such accidents in regional hospitals, but there is no register of the species involved. I am working on a campaign for the prevention of accidents in rural areas, integrated with the preservation of fragile areas with endemic species.

My statistical data about the epidemiological situation in Tucuman served as a database at the *Primeras Jornadas Nacionales de Capacitacion Cientifico Tecnicas Sobre Escorpionismo,* for Dr. Emilio Maury (Santiago del Estero), September 1998, to determine the amount of antivenom sent to my province.

I took an active part in a campaign for the prevention of accidents by designing pamphlets, posters, giving community talks, and working as a volunteer in the determination of accident-causing scorpions at public hospitals in Tucuman.

The study of the origin of the scorpion reproduction requires analysis. An important obstacle was the lack of bibliography and techniques for the preparation of material for cytogenetic studies in scorpions. Among the difficulties inherent to these studies is the rigidity of the chitin and mitotic division in the period between two molts. To solve this problem, I trained in a laboratory of human genetic research for two months, practicing standard techniques on scorpions. Later on, at the University of Buenos Aires, I obtained a tentative number of chromosomes, which will require further experimentation for confirmation.

The standard techniques used for extracting venom are manual and cutting of the telson (last part bearing the venom gland and the sting of scorpions). With Dr. Jose Corronca's assistance, I invented a technological device for the extraction of scorpion venom minimizing the risks to the technicians doing this work and making it possible to use the animal for more than one extraction.

The most exciting thing that has happened to me occurred in Fort Worth, Texas, at the 1998 International Science and Engineering Fair. The American Veterinary Medical Association granted me their Public Health Award. The American Association for the Advancement of Science also invited me to become a member.

At the International Science and Engineering Fair, in Philadelphia, in 1999, I was Kodak's First Place Award Winner for the best use of photography in collecting information and developing a science project. I was also recognized as one of the 2000 young world winners of the Millenium Dreamers Project, a global program sponsored by UNESCO that acknowledges community work. This award was given to boys and girls who made their communities a better place to live. I was selected for my contribution to the public health in my province for the prevention of scorpion accidents.

The fact that I was brought up in the midst of a family of naturalists, participated in exploration trips and species assessment, and listened to discussions about different biological theories made me a curious explorer of the natural world and its knowledge. The spirit of adventure present during field trips with my father, my brother, and sister climbing the Cardonal slopes, exploring rivers, and climbing 3500 meters of the Andean prairie also developed my sense of exploration.

Konrad Lorenz, Donald Griffen, Edward Wilson, and Lynn Margulis are the twentieth century researchers I admire. They are creative and innovative scientists who opened new fields in the knowledge of the natural world. Their books are a continuous source of inspiration to me.

My mother is my female role model. Although she is very busy at her research laboratory, she always finds time to give us all the love and support we need. It was my privilege that my mother, a biologist, supervised experimental techniques in gland venom histology and electron microscope studies.

I also particularly admire Lynn Margulis for her presence as a woman in the international scientific community. Her development of the imaginative theory of the endosymbiotic origin of mitochondria and other cellular organelles, enriches our cosmovision. Margulis is an example of generational continuity between parents and children in scientific work.

My participation in youth scientific and technological projects required a great effort from every point of view. The training allowed me to value knowledge critically as well as the importance of rigor and honesty in the collection, presentation, and elaboration of data. I think such experiences strengthen an individual and prepare you to undertake projects and to solve problems and make decisions. Besides widening the understanding of some sector of reality, the results of research are projected in services to the community. We young people discover that, above all, there are deep reasons why life is worth living. My advice to other girls and young women is to overcome minor and major difficulties. Never get discouraged even if circumstances may be adverse.

HALLIE LYNN
WOODWARD

*H*allie Woodward was born in June 1987. She was raised in Memphis, Tennessee, but now lives in a small town in Mississippi. She has always been interested in reading and writing, and especially likes to read scientific magazines such as National Geographic and Kids' Discover. Hallie has an enthusiastic personality along with a lot of strong determination. She is naturally curious and is not only interested in how something works, but why! This is why she loves science! Hallie is a strong math student and completed prealgebra credit in seventh grade and will be taking Algebra I in eighth grade. Hallie also writes a weekly article for the local newspaper.

ENVIRONMENTALIST

I have been interested in science ever since our move to Mississippi. My mother and I were driving to our new home, and I asked her how she knew which way to go. She told me that we were taking Highway 78, South. Okay, I knew what a highway was and I understood that the number 78 designated which one we were on, but how did my mom determine north, south, east or west? She told me those were directions. Still not understanding, I pressed her further to explain what were directions!

After settling into our new home, my school participated in a science fair. What could I do? That's when it hit me! What were directions? This led me to my first science fair project, which won first place in our school competition and second in the regional one. The science bug had bit me. I realized that there were forces in our universe that governed our lives. Each year thereafter, I participated in the science fairs. Not only did I learned from my projects, but also I made a lot of new friends and I learned from their projects as well. The more I learned, the more I was encouraged to further explore my investigations. Our world is so interesting and offers so many things to discover.

This past year, I studied the food chain, decomposition, and our changing world. Through these studies, I was able to place third in a NASA competition for my grade level. I also placed first in the Young Naturalist Awards conducted by the American Museum of Natural History. From these competitions, I have been able to go on a trip which broadened my perspective of our world, and I won scholarship money for college.

I became interested in my project because Desoto County is one of the fastest growing areas in the nation. Along with this exceptional growth, we have had our share of growing pains. How did this affect me? Well, the city did not have the infrastructure to supply utilities to all of the new residences during the winter. It got very cold! I was also greatly affected by the destruction of the woods behind my home, for I had enjoyed observing rabbits, fox, deer, owls, bluebirds, and many other creatures. When the developers started to bulldoze the land, I saw how these creatures ran for cover and literally lost their homes. For one entire summer, it seemed like we had no birds, frogs, or crickets. The quiet was deafening. Also, my family had a very hard time growing any flowers or new trees in our own lot. I wondered why. After much reading, experimenting, and investigating, I realized that the developers had also destroyed an unseen world. The world of saprophytes and the nutritious topsoil that plants need had been carried away by dump trucks. I realized that the first step, and the very last step of our world's food chain, had been destroyed by the developers.

Through these studies, I realized how wonderful the interactions of our world are in each organism's life. I realized that each creature and plant is very important. We are very important. Yet, we are also a very small part of the world. This discovery made me feel fantastic! How special each of us is.

I also realized that we are responsible for the condition of our world. I discovered that we had selfishly destroyed others' homes in order to build our own. We had not even attempted to save any part. We were totally unconcerned with the destruction we had caused to our immediate community of nature. Not only had we hurt plants, but other animals and ourselves, too.

I have tried to make a difference by recycling or reusing things in my home. I have talked to people in the community about being more aware of the environment. I have spoken to the mayor and other citizens about saving trees. Our local pharmacist has considered my suggestion of reusing plastic prescription bottles for patients' refills. I have helped my family plant trees, bushes, and flowers for the birds and butterflies. We have feeders, hummingbird nectar bottles, suet cages, and birdbaths. I have even put a bell on my cat's collar after witnessing the destruction of a mockingbird's nest and young. The most important thing that I have accomplished is to help my family make a compost bin. We use leftover food and paper scraps to fill the compost, which later goes into our flowerbeds. I have earthworms in my bins that also help our flowerbeds, and I can use them to go fishing! These are things that anyone of any age can accomplish at home.

The biggest obstacle that I have run into is expense. Our city has given up its recycling program because of expense. Developers would rather bulldoze the land than pay the expense of having a crew work around one hundred-year-old trees. Most of the political officials that I have spoken to are concerned more with expense and time than destruction of our environment.

I do have my supporters though. My parents and grandparents support my efforts. My neighbors have been adding feeders and birdbaths to their yards to replace the birds' natural habitats (trees). I have a lot of support from various members of the community. I have also gained support from my advanced science teacher, Ms. Bunyard. She has encouraged my "thinking out of the box" instead of forcing me to stay within bounds of ordinary lessons. She is willing to support me in all my efforts and is willing to spend time to talk to me about my interests. Ms. Denison, a former science teacher, also encourages my explorations and writing.

These two teachers always give me words of encouragement. Ms. Bunyard has e-mailed me over the summer about my interests—even though we are out of school. These teachers along with my family have helped me grow in my science work. I've also met newspaper reporters and editors who have introduced me to doctors, scientists, and museum directors. All of these people have helped me in my search for information and have encouraged me to broaden my explorations. Don't be afraid to talk to well-known adults. Many are happy to share their wisdom.

I will continue to look for more projects that will enhance my knowledge. I would especially like to find projects that make me more aware of my surroundings and myself. I believe that Florence Griffith Joyner was correct when she said, "If you wish to leave this world better than when you found it, you must care about others." I also believe Neil Simon when he said, "To have passion for life isn't only to wake up in the morning and hear birds singing, but it is to take the time to open the window to see where they are perched on the tree." These are two things I believe in strongly.

The advice I would give others is to make a difference. Be strong and do what interests you in life—no matter what anyone says. A lot of my friends who are girls cannot believe that I like to work in the soil and add to my compost pile. They think it is gross. A lot of the guys think I am either weird or just "trying to be like the guys." They are both wrong. When you realize how important the soil is to the food chain, along with decomposition, you realize that it is as important to life as the air that you breathe. Also, working in the soil and perspiring is not just a "guy" thing. How ridiculous! I like dressy dresses, lace, makeup, and perfume. I also like flowers, plants, animals, swimming, fishing, boating, and being in nature. I've also had a few teachers who will ignore my questions or my participation in class. They've listened to my questions and have told me that what I want to know is beyond the level I am studying. This frustrates me, but also makes me more determined to continue my studies. As young women, we must not be "put off." We must be determined and tenacious. Even if we have a question or comment that is of no interest to the rest of the class, we must refuse to be ignored. We must continue to look for the answers to our questions. Don't give up on your individual search for knowledge and success.

How do I plan on using my writing, science, and investigative skills? I am considering becoming an environmental lawyer or an environmental journalist. I could use all the skills I am currently working on to attain and use them in making the world—our world—a better place to live. As a woman, I want my world to be beautiful for myself, my current family and friends, and my future family. I will be able to earn a living and still do what makes me happy. As author Naomi Wolf says, "Push yourself a little further than you dare." I also believe in what author Anna Quindlen said, "If your success is not on your own terms, if it looks good to the world but does not feel good in your heart, it is not success at all." I want success.

ERICA ELIZABETH
YOUNGSTROM

*E*rica Elizabeth Youngstrom was born September 28, 1984, in Cleveland, Ohio. She now lives with her parents, sister, and brother in Shaker Heights, Ohio, where she attends Hathaway Brown School. Her many interests include playing the piano, horseback riding, reading, and working on a science project at NASA Glenn Research Center. Intellectual curiosity, a strong sense of motivation, and a love of problem solving help her excel in her areas of interest, particularly in the field of science. In the future, she would love to incorporate her knowledge of and interest in science into her career.

RESEARCH FOR NASA

From the day I learned of the chance to work on a project at Glenn Research Center through my school's research program, I knew that I wanted to use the opportunity to increase my knowledge of science and gain real-world experience. I wanted to pursue this scientific project because I found the problem, atomic oxygen erosion in space, to be extremely compelling and was excited by the prospect that I could make a difference in the world of science at such a young age. Books dealing with science and math, particularly those by Madeleine L'Engle, had already piqued my interest in this area. Though I was very young, even younger than the project's organizers had originally planned for the team members to be, I knew I had the support of my family, friends, and the people at school who made it all possible. As I began work on the project, meeting weekly with the supervising scientists and older team members, I felt almost overwhelmed by the amount of new knowledge and responsibility that was being given to me. Working in the real world was completely different from my experiences at school. I couldn't ask my teachers for help if I was stuck. I had to think through problems on my own or with my teammates. At first this was intimidating, but over time I have grown used to the challenge and come to think of it as a great benefit to me. This is only one of the reasons I am so grateful to have participated in the project.

After two years of work on the project, I can say that it has been an enormously positive experience. While it isn't always fun, it is always interesting and getting to work with NASA is an exciting opportunity. People often wonder how much fun it really is for my teammates and I to spend Friday afternoons and a significant part of our summers working full-time at NASA, but the idea that we're being productive and are on our way to making a real difference keeps us all going. We certainly don't feel that we're missing anything by spending some extra time working on the project. Being at NASA on such a regular basis gives me more than just experience in the labs; it gives me important knowledge of how to conduct myself in a professional environment. No matter what career path I one day choose to follow, this knowledge and work experience will always benefit me. Over the course of the project thus far, many memorable instances have arisen and have taught me valuable lessons.

One time, I was at NASA with my teammates working on an experiment as part of our project. As we were making observations and recording the results, we realized that the method we were using was inconsistent. Since the method had taken so long to develop, we were all frustrated that we would have to rethink it. Still, I was grateful for the fact that we had arrived at our decision through discussion and thought; this showed once again what a great team I was working with. In particular, my supervising scientist, Kim de Croh, has been a true role model for me. She has set an excellent example, which I will always remember. Never taking the easy way out, she makes sure that all the team's work is the highest quality possible before we move on to a new task. Most important, however, it has meant a lot to me to see a woman so dedicated to her scientific career.

Besides my teammates and supervisors, several other people have truly helped me to be where I am now. My parents have been a definite inspiration. My mother, a lawyer, demonstrates another instance of a woman following an exciting and demanding career path. My father's career as a doctor has shown me another use for my interest in science, which I may wish to consider as an occupation. Last, but certainly not least, Mrs. Patricia Hunt, the research coordinator at Hathaway Brown School, has done a tremendous amount for my teammates and me. She first presented me with the idea and opportunity to do this amazing project, and she has helped all of us balance the high commitment level of the project with our everyday lives and schoolwork.

One day, the results of our project may help to revolutionize areas of scientific experimentation. By making sure that the coating on the outside of space shuttles and satellites won't be eroded by single atoms of oxygen, making little bits of coating stick to the experiments and solar panels (which make the panels less efficient by blocking the Sun's rays), a greater number of valuable experiments may be conducted in space without problems. The knowledge that this may well be the result of the hours my teammates and I are putting in on the project is our ultimate satisfaction.

YOUNG WOMEN OF ACHIEVEMENT

Ages
Nineteen
and Older

Lourdes Cecilia Burt

Jenny Carlson

Ginger Denison

Amber Garber

Anne M. Hammerstrom

Carolyn Kaminski

Kari Kolton

Claretha Nichols

Susan Nieber

Alaina Joan Oas

Ying Wu

LOURDES CECILIA BURT

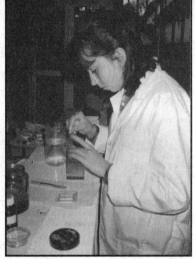

Lourdes Cecilia Burt was born June 29, 1982, in San Miguel de Tucuman, Argentina. Her parents are Nolberto Jorge Burt, a shopkeeper, and Maria Adela Moyano, a science teacher. She has two brothers, Christian and Martin. Lourdes is very quiet and curious. She likes investigating, reading, and intellectual thinking. She lives in Concepcion City, a very important administrative and commercial center of the area. She is currently attending the Colegio Nuestra de la Consolacion, where she also takes part in community activities. Her favorite subjects are biology and physical education.

INTERNATIONAL EXPERIENCES

When I was a child, I used to go with my mother to science and technology fairs because she is the coordinator of these fairs in my province. I would visit the projects of other children and teenagers, and became interested in working and participating in these events.

In 1995, I began participating in activities such as scientific camps, congress, and science and technology fairs. The following year, I took part as an exhibitor in the XXIII International Fair in Buenos Aires with the presentation "Young People in Science and Technology." During May 1997, together with other young people from my country and other countries, I participated in the Young People Regional Forum for Latin America and the Caribbean. In this event I received congratulations from the representative of the United Nations Program for the Environment, Mr. Rafael Rodriquez Capetillo. In September of that same year, I participated in *Ecovision*, a TV program in Mar del Plata, Argentina, that addresses environmental topics.

One of my greatest achievements was the opportunity to represent Argentina with my project, "Ecological Treasures, Behind the Traces of Citrus," at the fiftieth Intel International Science and Engineering Fair in Philadelphia, Pennsylvania. This achievement earned me, along with other young investigators, a presidential distinction given by our president Dr. Carlos Saul Menem. Participation in Philadelphia gave me the opportunity to share my experiences, interests, and culture with young people from all over the world. I also became aware that nothing is impossible if one dedicates one's time, effort, and perseverance. In my country, young people have to face many difficulties in developing our investigations. The main obstacle is the lack of economic resources.

Young people have to face many difficulties in developing investigations in my country. For example, there is a lack of professional tutors willing to serve as advisors, institutions often do not allow the access of young people to the world of science, and economical factors make it difficult to conduct investigations.

In 2000, I worked on a new project, "Soya's Drink: Improvement of its Nutritional Quality with the Incorporation of Lactic Bacteria," an investigation that aims to improve the quality of life for special groups of people with serious nutrition deficiencies. With this project I participated in the fifty-first Intel International Science and Engineering Fair in Detroit. With it I obtained fourth prize in microbiology in the ceremony for the grand awards.

My interest in this topic of investigation arose from the environmental characteristics of the area where I live which is ideal for the growing of citrus and Soya of excellent quality. They are both important in the production of food that is of high nutritional value. Currently, I am expecting to participate in the nineth International Environmental Olympics to be held in Turkey. All of these experiences have helped me to decide my vocational orientation. I have decided to begin a bachelor's degree in nutritional science at Santo Tomás de Aquino University.

In my country, Cecilia Grierson is admired for being the first woman to fight against discrimination, and she was able to study medicine obtaining her degree in 1889. At the international level, my role model is Mother Teresa from Calcutta for her life and service in helping the poor. Personally I want to thank my mother for stimulating me and others in developing scientific and technological thinking. My advice to young people is to overcome all obstacles because by having clear objectives, half of the work is already done.

JENNIFER
CARLSON

orn in Chicago, Illinois, February 17, 1982, Jennifer Carlson has lived in six states with her siblings, Christopher and Brittany; mother, Patricia; and father, Steven. Through her schooling, Jennifer has gained a broad perspective concerning the importance and diversity of knowledge. The most memorable experience of her youth occurred in fifth grade when she was introduced to mathematics through Theoni Pappas' book Joy of Mathematics. Since this experience, Jennifer has been extremely interested in mathematics and its applications outside the mathematical drills and memorization taught in the typical classroom. Her ability to see the beautiful but often neglected side of mathematics is the most pertinent trait characterizing her as a great student of mathematics. Jennifer attended the Indiana Academy for Science, Mathematics, and Humanities, and she now attends Dartmouth College and is studying mathematics. Jennifer's goals include earning a doctorate in mathematics and opening a private preparatory school.

DISCOVERING MATHEMATICS

When I was nine years old, my mother decided to have me tested for the advanced learning program at my elementary school. I failed the test—with flying colors. However, this failure was not necessarily a direct result of my mental capacities. Pathetically enough, my goldfish had died earlier that week, sending me into a fit of elementary-kid-style depression. Needless to say, this small occurrence cut me out of the advanced learning program my fourth-grade year.

Explaining the goldfish situation to my counselor, my mother attempted to have me tested again in fifth grade. Perhaps my mother had some sort of mother's intuition; I tested into the advanced learning program.

Although most kids were nervous the first day of that school year, I was a little more nervous because of the new class added to my schedule. Fifteen students and I strolled down a path toward a portable classroom. The floors inside creaked, not of antiquity, but of precariousness and instability. A plump woman with radiating strawberry blond hair greeted us. She stood at a podium at the front of the classroom, which was a rather odd sight for us fifth graders. After assuming that every student had been accounted for, she began a tiny speech.

"Hello, students. My name is Ms. Carter. This is the advanced learning program at Manzanita Elementary School," Ms. Carter said in a kind, coaxing voice. She described the mechanics of the classroom to which not one student paid attention and, with an abrupt change of manner, handed out a logic problem to every student that consisted of rearranging three rectangles into a specified shape.

"Now, I would like everyone to get out scissors and cut out these three rectangles. Think logically, and decide how you would solve the puzzle," Ms. Carter explained. She didn't act as though the required activity was difficult or easy; she was neutral about our abilities.

Some students were bold enough to jump up and retrieve scissors, quickly cutting the pieces for the problem at hand. Other students, like myself, sat in a kind of dumb shock, rereading the directions to make sure we had correctly understood. After a few minutes, I stood up and fetched a pair of scissors. At that time, I remember thinking this puzzle must be exceptionally difficult; at the same time I knew that if I could just think of something clever enough, the problem could be easily solved. After about fifteen minutes of finagling with the pieces, Ms. Carter caught on that the students were getting nowhere.

"Well, I didn't expect any of you would get this problem; this mind bender is actually very difficult." She flipped on the overhead projector, and we fixed our gazes on the light cast upon the blackboard. "Now, here is the solution." Without the shyness we had shown toward the pieces of paper, she quickly manipulated the papers into a viable solution.

"The problem I just gave you is a logic problem. More generally, it is a math problem." Some of the students wrinkled their noses in disgust. The mention of the word "math" sometimes provoked such responses in youngsters. "During the rest of the semester, we will be looking at different kinds of math. Some might be logical like this problem. Other activities might be different ways of looking at nature, like the Fibonacci sequence." She grabbed a piece of chalk and wrote the numbers 1, 1, 2, 3, 5, and 8 on the board in that order. "These are the first six numbers of the Fibonacci sequence. Can anyone see the pattern in these numbers?" She didn't wait for a response but continued as if no question were asked. "The pattern is, to get to the next number, you add the two preceding numbers. So, we start off with two 1's. Then, 1+1=2, which is the third Fibonacci number. To get the next number, we add 1+2=3. And so on." Our faces were momentarily captured, and then once again looked distracted. "This sequence is important; it appears in nature as the number of petals on a flower, the number of black keys on an octave piano, and many other places."

That semester we learned juicy tidbits of information from the *Joy of Mathematics*, which now has turned into my mathematical bible. We learned that math is beautiful, that math lies beyond the scope of "algebra" and "geometry." Even advanced subjects like calculus are dimmed in comparison to the simple, intriguing elements of mathematical thought we absorbed during that fifth-grade year. There was nothing difficult about anything we learned, nothing impossible to conceptualize, yet I am certain that every student who complains about the labors of math has never been exposed to these easily understandable mathematical truths. Mathematics never seemed dry to me after this class; I considered my "boring" math classes more as a drill than as "real mathematics."

A few days ago I was studying differential equations, and I realized that the solutions of certain types of differential equations are no more complicated than finding the root of a basic algebraic polynomial. Algebra might have passed for the most boring, listless, and rudimentary mathematics class that, if it didn't destroy a student's delight in math altogether, definitely replaced a once burning curiosity with a comparably apathetic interest. However, this simple course is all that is needed to solve difficult problems posed by engineers, biologists, and physicists. This amazing cleverness, circuitry, and beauty in mathematics was luckily shown to me early enough that it could be fully digested. Since fifth grade, I have fostered a love of mathematics that many people cannot fathom. Mathematics is not for the haughty researcher or the child-genius. Mathematics is for anyone simple-minded enough to see its beauty. As a child, I was able to grasp this side of mathematics, and I have been grateful ever since.

In relaying my experiences with mathematics, I cannot contend I am a mathematician nor have I done anything warranting any praise for my abilities. Having been admitted into Dartmouth College, I consider this acceptance to be one of my most important achievements; going to Dartmouth will enable me to truly embark upon my mathematical endeavors. I have written papers, won awards, and fulfilled my own desires by studying topics such as game theory and differential equations on my own. However, I feel that none of these traits, accomplishments, or activities really gets to the heart of my ambitions with mathematics. Rather, the passion with which I pursue these ambitions is the most important facet of any accomplishment I may achieve. Eva Peron once said, "Nothing can be accomplished without fanaticism." I believe that the passion and love for mathematics that has developed in me since fifth grade will, likewise, not only aid, but also force me to achieve my goals in mathematics. As advice to anyone with a dream, desire, or obstacle, I would recommend the above words of Eva be taken to heart. Undying passion and sustained persistence are not only essential in obtaining any goal, but rather they guarantee the manifestation of any person's ambitions.

GINGER
DENISON

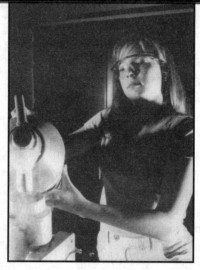

*G*INGER MICHELLE DENISON *was born April 21, 1978, to Don and Jody Denison. She spent her childhood in the woods of Paris, Tennessee, building forts and climbing trees with her younger brother, David. Their family moved to Greensboro, North Carolina, in 1989. Ginger's competitive nature became apparent with her participation in soccer, tennis, and track. Her desire to seek and conquer every challenge also translated to the classroom; math and science were her favorite subjects. Ginger's incredible curiosity, coupled with her love for science and nature, led her to the field of environmental chemistry. She chose to attend Furman University, where she excelled as a chemistry major and cocaptain of the track team. For the past two summers, she has conducted research at the Los Alamos National Laboratory. Ginger plans to pursue a Ph.D. in environmental analytical chemistry.*

TOXIC WASTE

Even before I could walk, I had a desire to explore the unknown. My parents encouraged me to be creative, allowing me to romp around the woods creating never ending adventures, fighting wars, chasing off dragons, and sailing the thundering seas. I always played the part of the lookout, climbing to the tops of the trees so I could see clear across the country.

I never stopped climbing trees or looking beyond small-town life. I wanted to go to college and have a successful career rather than marry after high school graduation, the goal of many of my school friends. I wanted to play soccer; since there were no girls' teams, I played with the boys. I wanted to study science and math without being ridiculed. When I was twelve, we moved to Greensboro, North Carolina. I left my wooded trails behind, but I took my determination with me.

Determination is one of the key elements of chemistry. Chemistry is a fascinating field, full of phenomena still unknown to us. As an undergraduate at Furman University, I was given the opportunity to work at Los Alamos National Laboratory during the summer months. I accepted this offer and took off for the west. My research in Los Alamos focused on one aspect of the Hanford project.

The Hanford waste site, located in the state of Washington, is a primary storage site for hazardous and nuclear wastes. The site consists of 177 tanks containing over 55 million gallons of waste left over from plutonium production during the Cold War. The most favorable treatment for clean up of this site is vitrification, where the waste is placed inside large glass logs.

However, the waste contains chromium (III), a metal that makes glass brittle. Therefore, the chromium (III) must be removed prior to vitrification. The easiest way to remove the chromium is to dissolve it in water, then wash it out of the waste before placing it in the glass log. Chromium (III) is not soluble (it cannot be dissolved in water), but chromium (VI) is soluble. Therefore, the chromium must be oxidized from III to VI so it can be removed.

My project focused on oxidizing (removing electrons from) the chromium (III) using hydrogen peroxide. I used hydrogen peroxide because it is readily available, environmentally safe, and the reaction with chromium happens quickly. Other scientists are trying to use high temperature and pressure, but the radioactive waste is unstable at those conditions and may be unsafe. With the help of my advisor, Tony Arrington, I worked on characterizing the kinetics of the reaction, which explains how fast the oxidation reaction from chromium (III) to chromium (VI) occurs.

One discovery I made was that the older the tank waste is, the slower the reaction. This is important, since the waste is now over forty years old. Over time, the chromium (III) in the tank bonds together to make long chains that are less reactive. Now we can predict the structure of chromium in the tanks and use that information to try new techniques.

Other important conclusions involve the pH of the tank waste. The waste is very alkaline (pH of around 13). My experiments showed that the higher the pH, the slower the reaction. I also conducted experiments to see how temperature affects the reaction rate; in general, reactions proceed faster as the temperature increases. This was true for the oxidation of chromium. I determined the energy it takes to start the reaction to be very low. This means the reaction occurs quickly at room temperature.

During my time at Los Alamos, I have met and worked with many eminent and inspiring scientists, including two Nobel Laureates, on universal environmental concerns. As a lab researcher, I have been exposed to aspects of the scientific world uninvestigated in the classroom; I have come to realize the importance of politics and interdisciplinary cooperation, as well as the impact of public perception. Working at the lab has also made me aware of the issues involved in a male-dominated field; the ratio of men to women in Los Alamos was almost nine to one. Often it was difficult for the scientists to take me seriously; more difficult was finding a women's restroom!

Obstacles like this in my life have only served to strengthen my conviction and my dedication to science. The courage to accomplish great things in one's life starts with very small steps.

Believing in your own ideas was my start. Simple things, such as raising my hand in class to answer a question, have enhanced my self-esteem. It's often the big changes that force you to be your own person. When I moved from the small rural town of Paris, Tennessee, to the seemingly immense area of Greensboro, North Carolina, the transition from gravel roads and friendly faces to four-lane highways and impersonal contact was rough. My clothes were not the chic brands, my hair was too frizzy, and there was a wild rumor throughout school saying I was the new French exchange student (apparently I had not clarified that I was from Tennessee).

It did not take long for me to find my place. I knew what my strengths were and I focused on them; I was a good math student, so I joined the Math Counts team, and I had loved the soccer league, so I signed up for a local team. Most important, I had support all the way. I was willing to share with my parents, teachers, and friends any troubles I was experiencing, rather than keeping them locked inside.

The most important role models in my life have been the people with whom I have everyday contact. Two female math teachers recognized my gift for the subject and helped me develop it. My father always urged me to follow my dreams, no matter my heritage, the color of my hair, or my gender. My mother taught me that while being successful is an accomplishment, I should always have fun in life. She has given me the gift of laughter, which is a blessing in the face of stress and conflict. I also greatly admire many prominent females from both the past and present. Marie Curie opened the doors for female scientists, showing the world that gender is no measure of scientific intelligence. Eleanor Roosevelt and Elizabeth Dole are other amazing women from whom any person can learn. Both have successful husbands and a happy home life, but never played the part of solely a homemaker. I only hope that I can someday have as many accomplishments as these ladies have achieved.

To this point in time, I am proud of my accomplishments. To others pursuing their dreams, I wish them luck. Remember never to take anyone for granted; every person has his or her own story, and that story could change your life. Be bold. Be creative. Every now and then, climb a tree and get a new viewpoint. Some of my best decisions have been made among the branches. Take time for yourself, and learn to say no. That was one of the hardest things for me to do, but I have never regretted taking a quiet time-out. Make friends with everyone. This includes the man at the coffee stand, the five-year-old next door, and the school janitor. Most important, dream hard and play harder. One can never grow up too fast.

AMBER
GARBER

*A*mber Garber is a graduate student in molecular marine biology at The University of Southern Mississippi. She won Best Student Poster Award at the Annual International Conference and Exposition of the World Aquaculture Society held in Sydney, Australia (May 1999), and Best Student Presentation Award at the Fifty-Second Annual Meeting of the Gulf and Caribbean Fisheries Institute held in Key West, Florida (November 1999). These presentations described Garber's genetic research, a baseline description of a portion of the mitochondrial DNA of wahoo from the northern Gulf of Mexico and Bimini, Bahamas. Born in Ohio October 5, 1975, Amber is the daughter of Dr. Gary and Tooie Garber. She was taught and strives to live by the virtues of honesty, integrity, personal responsibility, and hard work. Her interest in science began at a young age when she and her two siblings assisted in their parents' veterinary practice.

THE GREAT WAHOO

My personal accomplishments in science cannot be warranted as mine and mine alone. The two most recently recognized accomplishments in my life were winning the Best Student Poster Award at the Annual International Conference and Exposition of the World Aquaculture Society (May 1999) held in Sydney, Australia, and the Best Student Presentation Award at the Fifty-Second Annual Meeting of the Gulf and Caribbean Fisheries Institute held in Key West, Florida (November 1999). At those two meetings I presented the results of pioneering research on the genetics of the wahoo, a highly prized offshore species of fish. We sequenced pieces of mitochondrial DNA containing portions of two genes, three transfer RNAs, and a noncoding region (control region) of the wahoo. This research was conducted in the molecular laboratory at the Gulf Coast Research Laboratory (GCRL) in Ocean Springs, Mississippi.

Little is known about the biology and life history of this spectacular sport fish. When I began graduate school at The University of Southern Mississippi in May 1998, Jim Franks (Fisheries Research Biologist) and Nikola Garber (graduate student) infused me with excitement related to their work on the wahoo. Nikola, working on completing her master's thesis, subsequently began teaching me the molecular laboratory techniques necessary to continue the ancillary wahoo project. I began to participate in the collections of genetic samples from wahoo at Northern Gulf fishing tournaments, as well as from Bimini, Bahamas. The science team in the Bahamas was noteworthy. Jim, unable to attend, designated my parents and David Geter (a special friend and Ph.D. candidate) to assist Nikola and myself with sample collection.

Once collected, samples must undergo lengthy, intricate laboratory procedures designed to unlock their "science." The following summarizes our continuing research. Mitochondria, otherwise known as the powerhouse of the cell due its role in respiration (giving our bodies energy), contains its own unique type of DNA (the mitochondrial genome). Mitochondrial DNA is different because its DNA sequence changes at a faster rate than nuclear DNA. More specifically, within the mitochondrial genome lies the control region, a DNA sequence that does not code for a gene or protein and can, therefore, also change parts of its DNA sequence faster than other parts of the already quickly evolving mitochondrial genome. Due to its variability, the control region can be a useful tool in helping understand the structure of a population of fish. For example, it might demonstrate that the fish found off the coast of Mississippi are very closely related to the same type of fish found off the coasts of the surrounding states. If a certain type of fish was declared overfished in Mississippi, fishery managers could use research to determine if regulations on commercial and recreational fisheries are necessary in order to give stocks time to rebuild.

We obtained mitochondrial DNA sequences from the wahoo tissue samples collected (Gulf of Mexico; Bimini, Bahamas). In these sequences we identified three transfer RNAs (tRNA), which are short pieces of DNA in a cloverleaf configuration, necessary during translation. We used the small pieces of sequences on either side of the control region to make primers. This is possible because each wahoo should have the same tRNA sequence as every other wahoo. We used these primers to amplify and sequence the wahoo control region. We aligned all the sequences and were then able to identify portions of the DNA that are conserved between different animals, especially different fish species. As an example, one small piece of wahoo DNA was the same as a small piece of trout DNA and very close to a piece found in sturgeon. This was done as part of a characterization of the control region of the wahoo control region DNA as it compares to that of other fish.

Research in my chosen field continues to be a rewarding experience. Fishermen and spectators frequently ask questions at fishing tournaments about our work with wahoo, which allows dissemination of past discoveries, stimulates continued interest and support, and highlights applicability of scientific research. Present progress with wahoo genetics has fallen victim to the academic villains, time constraints and funding; however, we would like to continue in the future.

Actually, my interest in science began at an early age. When my sister and I were very young, my father would allow us to travel on some of his large-animal veterinary rounds. There, he would take all the materials needed out of a large black bag, providing a perch from which my sister and I would observe his ministrations. As I aged, I was allowed to assist in the clinic where my mother worked as his animal technician. The science involved in diagnosis and treatment was fascinating, but I knew I would be better suited in a different facet of science. My interest in both math and science increased in high school while in the classrooms of two gifted educators, Mr. Clifford Bronson and Mr. Robert Fowles. Once again, however, I found science more exciting, as I ". . . ate the elephant a bite at a time" (Mr. Fowles's classroom slogan to promote continual assimilation and retention). Although it did not work for many of my classmates, the more I studied the more intrigued I became with science.

As high school came to a close, independence, career indecision, and college loomed on the horizon. My eighteenth summer began as a travel escort for my sister, as she motored eighteen hours to the GCRL where she would be taking classes and working for Jim Franks. She was passionately interested in marine biology, which at the time, was of little interest to me. My short stay provided insight and enjoyment, prompting a return at the end of the summer to help her finish her work before the long trek home. She gave me the most "coveted" task, weighing and measuring the wet and dry weights of preserved fish stomachs!

That fall, I entered Bowling Green State University in Ohio, knowing I would like to pursue a degree in science, but not knowing where I might fit. Through an affiliation with GCRL at Bowling Green, I returned (with my sister) the summer after my freshman year to take Oceanography and Marine Ichthyology. I also returned the following two summers at which time I collaborated on research projects, was a teaching assistant for the marine ichthyology class, and worked as a technician in Histopathology and Fisheries. Through my undergraduate studies, I was most interested in genetic and cancer research. I chose to work on a genetics project for my masters and began graduate studies at GCRL just two weeks after college graduation. Currently, I am working on my master's thesis, the development of a genetic tag for red snapper to be used as a tool in stock assessment and enhancement endeavors under the supervision of Dr. Ken Stuck.

There are many things I have learned while maturing and striving to achieve. My parents instilled in me the focus to always strive to be honest, function with integrity, take personal responsibility, and work hard. My advice to anyone in any field of endeavor is to try to live by these virtues. When striving to achieve, you may not get there at first, not necessarily because you are not qualified, but because the criteria at that time does not fit you. Do not give up; if you strive to achieve, you will, and you will be recognized for it eventually.

Although my family is not perfect, to me it could never be better. If possible, look to obtain strength through your family. I look to my mother for strength. She tried extremely hard to make us happy while canning food, preparing dinners, and working for my father. I look to my father for strength. He spurred us to excel intellectually while helping my mother care for us and prepare us for the world. I look to both of them to see togetherness and how they sacrificed by always taking us with them to meetings or on vacations that could easily have been just their own private getaway. I look to my sister for strength. She has taught me that no matter what others think, it is what you think about yourself that truly matters. I look to my younger brother, Race, for strength. He taught me that humor in the form of sarcasm and wit can be useful when others are being condescending or malicious. They have taught me the most important lessons in life. For those lessons, I will love them forever and strive to create an environment around me as loving and giving as the one in which I was nurtured.

I have found that it is not possible to show everyone "this" world, but one must try—for without an attempt, one can never achieve. Life is interaction.

ANNE M. HAMMERSTROM

*A*nne was born November 17, 1982, and has one older brother and two dogs. Her interests include field hockey, skiing, music from around the world, cosmology, and reading. Some of her favorite activities at school are helping to run the Asian Awareness Association, writing for her school's literary magazine, and competing in a team engineering competition. She lives in Hudson, Ohio, and attends school at Hathaway Brown. Anne cites her enthusiasm for learning and relentless curiosity as the personality traits that most interested her in science and technology.

LEARNING TO APPRECIATE THE SCIENCES

For the last few years, I have had the opportunity to work on two different science research projects through the science Research Seminar Program at my school. The first is an astrophysics project that two other students and I have worked on in the Physics Department at Case Western Reserve

University. Under the guidance of our supervising scientist, we used temperature anisotrophy data in the cosmic microwave background radiation to learn more about the beginning conditions of the universe. We intend to continue our exploration of astrophysics by possibly doing a project related to dark matter. The other project I am involved with, called PEACE (acronym for Polymer Erosion and Contamination Experiment), is another group project consisting of a few other students, two teachers, and three research professionals from the Electrophysics Department at NASA's Glenn Research Center. PEACE is a materials durability experiment designed to test a model predicting a correlation between the polymer structure on the surface of space shuttles and the rate at which the polymer is eroded by atomic oxygen in low-Earth orbit. I consider myself to be extremely lucky to be working on two fascinating projects with so many great scientists, engineers, and students.

Surprisingly, before the last few years, I have never really thought of myself as a "science" person. History and English were my favorite subjects at school, and I actually used to fall asleep in math and science classes. This changed about four years ago. Because I have always loved to read and ask "Why?" questions, I started reading nonfiction science books. One of the first books I picked up in eighth grade was *In Search of Schrodinger's Cat* by John Gribben, which is about the fundamental strangeness of quantum mechanics. I was intrigued and continued to read about anything that caught my curiosity like *Hyperspace* by Michio Kaku or *Black Holes and Time Warps* by Kip Thorne, or any of several books by Stephen Jay Gould. In these books I found a science unlike what was taught at school. As my imagination began to work, I came to see a limitless beauty in science, from the flurried serendipity of subatomic structures to the massive grace of the galaxies.

Even though I loved to read about science, I still thought the science I was taught in school was boring. This changed in ninth grade when I started at Hathaway Brown School. In biology, physics, and chemistry, I found both enthusiastic teachers and interesting subject material. And as I saw how elegantly math could be used to describe science, I began to appreciate and like math more as well. My sophomore year, the director of the research program at my school, Patricia Hunt, asked if I would like to do a research project. At first I didn't want to because I had previous negative experiences with science research and science fairs in middle school. I was also concerned about having enough time in my schedule to do well in school and participate in athletics. But more than anything else, I was worried that I did not have enough of a science and math background to be able to conduct meaningful research. Mrs. Hunt continued to encourage me, and seeing some of my friends participate in the research program encouraged me as well. Getting involved in the research program was probably one of the best decisions I have ever made.

I got into the astrophysics project mainly because I love the concepts and questions involved. How did the universe begin? How will it end? How soon will it end? What is the universe made of? This project let me do what I like best: indulge my curiosity about the universe. Not only have I increased my familiarity with the field of astrophysics, but I have also had the opportunity to work with great teammates and three very patient supervising scientists.

I got involved with the PEACE project a little later that same year for three reasons. First, it was a chance to explore something much more experimental than the astrophysics project. Second, working on an experiment that would go into space appealed to me. And third, the problem of atomic oxygen erosion was fascinating to me. Most people usually think of space as a vacuum, but the presence of this erosive atomic oxygen has presented a considerable materials degradation concern for anyone operating any type of craft in low-Earth orbit. The PEACE experiment we hope will, ultimately, lead to more durable polymer coatings on satellites and space stations.

Luckily, the projects I participated in did not require extensive previous knowledge. Thanks to the patience and willingness of my supervising scientists, being enthusiastic, dependable, and hardworking was much more important. Again, the support of the research professionals, the research program at Hathaway Brown School, and my family made my participation possible. The only obstacle I really encountered was finding time in my schedule for the projects as well as participating in athletics, other extracurricular activities, and, of course, homework!

If I had a chance, I would certainly do it all again. Besides the enjoyment of gaining knowledge, I feel like I have benefited in a host of other ways. Teamwork, time management, and perseverance (even when I can't get equipment to work!) are just a few of the practical skills I believe I have honed. I have developed confidence in what I say and write. I have learned to see how each day's work is part of a longer and more complex process.

I honestly cannot think of a time in my life when I have had more fun working with all the mentors, teachers, and students who have been part of the two projects.

My most admired female role model is my mother, an outstanding professional, artist, thinker, and mother. I also immensely admire many of the women I have come in contact with who manage to successfully juggle teaching, science, or research as well as their families. Then again, I admire the many men I know who do the same thing.

To any girls or young women who may be struggling with whether to go into math, science, or technology—do not be sucked in by societal stereotypes of what women can and cannot do. Some less enlightened individuals of my acquaintance have expressed amazement that I would pursue science projects (admittedly, this may be more because I am a "humanities" person, than because I am a young woman). Luckily, most people react favorably and encouragingly to finding out that I participate in two research projects. But basically, if you've really found something you love and want to do, persevere and pursue your goals. What does it matter what anyone else thinks as long as you're doing what you love? The most important advice I can give is not to be afraid to try new things, be ambitious, and work hard to achieve your goals.

CAROLYN
KAMINSKI

Carolyn Kaminski was born December 19, 1982, in Cleveland, Ohio. She has an older sister, and a younger sister and brother. Carolyn attended preschool and kindergarten at Jewish Day Nursery and went on to St. Gregory the Great School until the sixth grade. After sixth grade, Carolyn transferred to Hathaway Brown School where she stayed through high school. During high school, Carolyn ran cross-country and track and played basketball. In school, Carolyn participated in Gold Key, Model United Nations, the World Affairs Club, Research Seminar, and Executive Council. She likes to work problems out and practice theories to perfection, whether on the courts or in the classroom.

EXPERIMENTS IN SPACE

As a child, my father used to take me to the different museums in Cleveland. My favorites were the Natural History Museum, where I could see the dinosaur bones and the different types of rocks. My other favorite was the NASA Museum. I would visit this museum at least once a month to see the model spacecrafts and photos from space, as well as videos on many different topics.

At Hathaway Brown, my eighth-grade teacher really got me interested in science. The course was in earth science, and I learned about the many types of rocks, the different star cycles, and the various prehistoric time periods. That year I made a wind tunnel for the science fair and tested different wing angles for lift. The research was difficult, but it taught me a lot about experimentation.

During my sophomore year, I had the same teacher for research class, and she introduced me to a project at NASA. I was immediately excited by this opportunity because it allowed me to solve real problems and work with different classmates and professionals at NASA.

I worked on this project throughout my sophomore, junior, and senior year, as well as in the summers. At first I was a little intimidated working with older students and professional scientists, but after my first outing to NASA, I immediately felt comfortable. The professional scientists knew a lot about my project, and they were willing to share their knowledge with me. They also told me about different projects they were working on, and the scientific concepts behind them. I learned as much by hands-on experimentation as I did from asking the scientists questions.

The most exciting part of this experiment so far is that it is flying on two different missions. First, it will travel to the International Space Station, where it will stay for a couple of years. I will not be in high school to see the second flight, but I am looking forward to seeing other students carry on the research that my team has worked on.

KARI
KOLTON

*K*ari Kolton is a sophomore at Carroll College in Waukesha, Wisconsin, majoring in marine biology and minoring in politics with an emphasis on nonprofit organizations and grant writing. Kari plans to transfer to Hawaii Pacific University to complete her degree. She was born July 23, 1981, in Milwaukee, Wisconsin. Since her freshman year in high school, Kari has volunteered at the Wisconsin Lake Schooner Education Association, assisting in teaching some of their numerous educational programs. She spends most of her free time café hopping and going to concerts with friends on Milwaukee's eclectic East Side. Her perseverance, passion, and a willingness to do everything she can to achieve her goals will one day make her a wonderful marine biologist.

SUMMER AT SEA

My goal to become a marine biologist is more like a dream evolving into reality. During my high school career, I was blessed with several opportunities that contributed to this reality. The patience and perseverance I learned there has helped me in other situations. The people who have helped me to succeed in these programs have taught me great lessons in kindness and selflessness. Participating in these programs has provided me with a network of resources and valuable insight into my career choice.

During the summer of 1998, I had the opportunity to participate in an extraordinary program for high school students called the High School Marine Biology (HSMB) program through the John G. Shedd Aquarium in Chicago. The program included thirty students and a seven-day excursion aboard Shedd's eighty-foot research vessel, *The Coral Reef II*, in Bimini, Bahamas. Participants were divided into three groups of ten, and then assigned a week in July for the voyage to the Bahamas. Before the trip everyone met at Shedd for two weeks of intense classes, to learn all that was needed for the adventure. Three instructors went through everything from physical and chemical properties of the ocean to teamwork.

Once in the Bahamas, boat chores, hard work, and salty sea air left us exhausted by the end of each day. We snorkeled at several different sites, with as many as four dives in one day. Activities included such things as comparing a coral reef community during the day with one at night. Field study projects were also required of each student, with a partner, with as many as five projects going on simultaneously. My partner and I conducted a plankton survey. Plankton are small, usually microscopic animals and plants. We concentrated on animal plankton, called zooplankton. Our objective was to discover which species were more abundant at a given time and location. The hardest part of the project was the microscope work, identifying and classifying the plankton. We found a greater variety of zooplankton offshore at night, as compared to offshore during the day, and onshore during both day and night. The other research projects included a beach seine survey, a tidepool survey, day and night community comparison, and marine debris assessment. One of my favorite activities was algae collection. Each individual was assigned to find a specific species of algae. I was told that mine was the hardest to find, so I was determined to make this mission a success. The scientific name for my algae was *caulpera sertularioides f. farowii*, or commonly known as caulpera. I did find my algae, however it resided near very territorial fish. It was quite an interesting task gathering the strands I needed. Once back on the boat we dried and pressed our algae so we could keep it. Another exciting thing was being able to celebrate my seventeenth birthday on the boat. This entire experience not only provided me with a wealth of new information but great new friends, too.

Following the field experiences, class resumed at Shedd. We had three days to complete our research projects, along with a full report. Additionally we prepared a skit and our project presentations for an evening seminar for our families, friends, and teachers.

The application process for participating in this program was almost as challenging as the program itself. There were pages of questions asking about the science classes I had taken and the final grade for each of them, the activities I am involved in, and so on. It also involved two essays about why I wanted to participate in HSMB and what I expected to gain, as well as explaining the cartoon character I felt I was most like. I also needed two recommendations, one from my science teacher and the other from another teacher or counselor. A swimming test was also required to verify my ability to perform several tasks, such as swimming underwater for twenty-five yards and treading water for five minutes. Additionally, the application included a form for my parents to complete, and I had to include a current transcript of all the classes I had taken up to applying for the program. After completing the entire application, I was called for an interview. The final decision was made after the interview. The thirty selected students and their parents were then invited to Shedd for an evening orientation.

I first applied for the program in 1997 and made it up to the interview. In the weeks to follow I was devastated I was not selected, although I now understand why. During that summer I was able to participate in two other programs, which would have not been possible if I had been in the Bahamas. The first was the shooting of a Jason Project video about aquatic life in the Great Lakes. Those involved with the video did water-quality testing in the Milwaukee River, which flows into Lake Michigan. The aquatic life present in the lakes was displayed in aquariums at the Wisconsin Lake Schooner Education Association. The video created was also shown to students nationwide. This opportunity strengthened my relations with the staff at WLSEA as well as allowed me to meet local representatives of the Jason Project.

A crew of seven students, including peers from my high school and myself, won a contest to do research aboard the Great Lakes Research Facility's (now known as the WATER Institute) vessel. Our objective was to study mysis migration in Lake Michigan. Mysis are a type of zooplankton that migrates at night, from the bottom of the lake to the thermocline to feed. No research had been done on them since the 1970s. Scientists were worried that the presence of the zebra mussels would be affecting the mysis, because they are both filter feeders. At the conclusion of the project, my peers and I completed a multimedia presentation that was given to the scientists at the institute. This project allowed me to network with a multitude of scientists who had the opportunity to witness my passion for the water and its contents firsthand. The following year, I reapplied for HSMB with all this experience "under my belt," and the rest is history.

The individuals who helped me accomplish all of these things are phenomenal. My sixth-grade science teacher, Mrs. Robin Rafaelidys, was instrumental in helping me to discover my love for science and, consequently the ocean. In the environment of a new school and knowing no one, Mrs. R. was amazing. Without her I know I would not have made it emotionally and spiritually through sixth grade. I received a $500 scholarship from Shedd, however I still needed about $1,400 to cover the cost of airfare, a passport, and train fare to and from Chicago on the pre- and posttrips. My high school science teacher was able to find full funding for me!

There is nothing I could do or say that would adequately thank those who have so kindly helped me. Helping me accomplish my goal was enough for them.

I would love to do each of these experiences over again, especially going to the Bahamas every summer to do research. I learned so much, beyond any of my expectations. I knew going into HSMB that careers dealing with the ocean, marine biology, oceanography, and so on are highly competitive and the pay is not the best. I now have a better idea about the job market, and I know this is something I will not be doing for the money. Thanks to the classes before our excursions, I have so much more information and appreciation for the ocean and its fragile ecosystems. Most important, HSMB reaffirmed my desire to become a marine biologist.

Following my heart has led me to these opportunities. There is no certain book or author who has inspired my interests. However, now that I know this is what I need to do with my life, I love to see, read, and apply the information I am gathering about the ocean's life as much as possible. I truly believe my calling in life is to in some way help save and conserve our world's oceans. The challenge in each of our lives is to recognize the calling. My first year of college was very hard, and I do not expect the second one to get any easier. The costs as well as the classes are becoming increasingly difficult. It is the perseverance and passion for what I know I will be able to accomplish five or ten years from now that get me through each day and will continue to do so. I am lucky to have parents who encourage me in what I want to do not what is "in the family." It is important to do what will make you happy, because it is your life, and you are the one who has to live it.

CLARETHA
NICHOLS

*C*laretha Nichols was born October 9, 1978, in Moss Point, Mississippi, a small town located along the Gulf of Mexico. She grew up in a middle-class family with her parents Posey and Avis. Her parents taught her the importance of education, family, and moral integrity. This background allowed her to excel through grade school and helped her become valedictorian of her graduating class at Moss Point High School.

Currently, Claretha is attending The University of Southern Mississippi where she is pursuing a career in biochemistry. She hopes to attend medical school to become a physician and would also like to conduct medical research in the future. Her mother and grandmother's deaths from heart disease have inspired her desire to pursue a career in medical science in order to improve the quality and longevity of human life. Claretha has attributed her success to her faith, her hard work and determination, and the support from her family and friends. She hopes to someday accomplish her goal of curing brain cancer.

A CURE FOR CANCER

In April 2000, I was awarded a prestigious Merck scholarship, which offered me $25,000 and an opportunity to work at Merck pharmaceutical laboratories for two summers.

Merck and Company is a leader in pharmaceutics and has developed a number of revolutionary drugs and vaccines that have saved millions of lives. Working at such a prestigious pharmaceutical company, I hope to gain insight in medical research and begin designing a few medical innovations of my own.

I am honored that Merck's contributions to my education will not only benefit me but also other students at The University of Southern Mississippi (USM) as well. Merck will donate $10,000 to the Chemistry and Biochemistry Department that will be used for scholarships and establishing a chemical modeling tutorial program. This contribution will encourage other students like me to pursue a career in science.

I discovered my passion for science and research in high school. While watching *The Manhattan Project: The Making of the Atomic Bomb* in my tenth-grade chemistry course, I was fascinated with Albert Einstein and his ingenious postulate—*energy equals the mass of an object times the speed of light squared*—that led to the making of the atom bomb. It was this small idea, which many scientists at the time believed to be untrue, that changed the lives of millions forever. I, too, wanted to have the same impact Albert Einstein has had on science, which, for me, could only be achieved by doing research.

It was not until illness struck my family that I realized my research career should involve medicine. My grandmother died of heart disease and my great-grandmother developed Alzheimer's. Both of these women were instrumental in my mental growth and development. My grandmother was a strong, charismatic woman who always encouraged me to dream the impossible. She came from poor surroundings, had little education, and never had a chance to make her career dreams come true. Yet, she encouraged me to work hard and not allow anything to stop me from attaining what I wanted in life. My great grandmother also encountered many hardships, but she encouraged me to use the opportunities available to me that were not afforded to her while she was growing up. I can still hear her voice saying, "I want you to go to school and do all the things I never could do." I have vowed to her and to myself that I will do just that by being a medical researcher.

I have embarked upon many research experiences already. The summer after high school graduation, I studied the antifungal properties of the cutleaf daisy at The University of Southern Mississippi. My work involved dissolving the ground-up plant in a number of organic solvents, purifying the compounds that dissolved, and determining if the dissolved compound exhibited antifungal activity. Although the compound could not be isolated during that summer, I did prove that a dissolved compound mixture previously deemed inactive was, in fact, active.

In January 1998, I began working with Dr. James Minn at USM studying the rate at which a number of household goods, including cooking oils and plastics, degrade. This allowed us to begin designing a technique that would slow the degradation process and extend the shelf life of household products.

During the summer of 1999, I worked at John Hopkins University in Washington, D.C., confirming the involvement of two proteins in brain cancer. The confirmation of these two proteins, has, in part, provided the researchers at John Hopkins with a method for inhibiting the growth of brain cancer.

Currently, I am studying the soybean chloroplast DNA polymerase, a protein involved in the reproduction of plant DNA. During the course of this research project, I plan to isolate an entire cDNA clone of it—which is simply a molecule of DNA made from RNA—and determine its genetic sequence.

All of these research experiences have been invaluable. They have shown me the basic principles behind conducting research, given me insight on how scientists approach problem solving, and prepared me for the research endeavors to come. Although not all of these research experiences have been in medicine, they have been instrumental in helping me attain my goal of becoming a medical researcher.

If time and resources were unlimited, I would cure all diseases in the world. Since this is not the case, my goal is to become a neuroscientist, and a team of researchers and I will work to cure brain cancer. Brain cancer is one of the most malignant and aggressive forms of cancer and can have debilitating effects on its victims. Curing it will not only save lives but may, perhaps, bring scientists closer to curing all forms of cancer. Thus, by winning this scholarship, I have moved one step closer to finding a cure for cancer.

SUSAN
NIEBUR

*S*usan Mahan Niebur was born April 13, 1973, to Pat and Maury Mahan, both educators. Susan grew up in Jackson, Mississippi, where she was a Girl Scout, soccer player, active member of her church youth group, and captain of her MathCounts, Challenge Bowl, and Quiz Bowl teams. Susan was part of the first class of fourth-grade students in the Academic and Performing Arts Complex and continued in the advanced classes through high school. This half-day magnet program and annual math and science competitions kept her scientific interest alive and growing and taught her leadership, perseverance, and the rewards of dedicated study. Her single-minded pursuit of excellence for both herself and her team was excellent preparation for her later research work in college and graduate study. She is currently a graduate student researcher at Washington University in St. Louis, Missouri, analyzing cosmic ray data collected by NASA's Advanced Composition Explorer spacecraft.

COSMIC RAYS

"Mom! Dad! There's going to be a science fair at school!" I was so excited the day they announced the first-ever science fair at McLeod Elementary. Finally, we would have the chance to build our own science projects and compete against other kids in the whole fourth grade. Since I was interested in learning how electricity works, my dad and I built a circuit using a nine-volt battery, wire, and a tiny light bulb. After some thought about what question I wanted to answer, I cut the wire in two and wrapped each end around a piece of metal. Then I completed the circuit with several different materials (a nail, a brass screw, a pencil, and a chicken bone) to determine which would best conduct electricity and light the bulb. My hypothesis was that the nail would conduct electricity well and the chicken bone would not. I was not completely right (the chicken bone did conduct electricity), but I learned the scientific method: formulate an interesting question, make a hypothesis, design a test, perform an experiment, and draw conclusions from the data. The research and presentation skills I used for the judges are the same ones that I rely on every day in my research into the nature of cosmic rays and the interstellar medium.

Galactic cosmic rays are atomic nuclei produced in distant stars that have traveled thousands of light years through the galaxy at such high velocities that the very electrons have been stripped away from the nuclei. NASA instruments such as the Cosmic Ray Isotope Spectrometer on the Advanced Composition Explorer spacecraft detected these particles for my doctoral dissertation. A Ph.D. in physics requires two years of graduate physics classes, a qualifying exam, and contribution of new research to the field. In my research, I have written and used computer programs to identify the elements detected, to compare abundances of sub-iron elements and their isotopes, and to determine isotopic ratios that can tell us whether these particles encountered shock waves produced by a supernova explosion during their journey to Earth. This work, which can help us understand the nature of interstellar space, has required all of my scientific skills, including formulating an interesting question, designing tests, performing data analysis, and drawing reasonable conclusions that will stand up to questions by experts in the field—the same skills I learned in the science fair!

Science fairs taught me a lot about independence and how much one can achieve by starting with a well-laid plan. I also learned the importance of meeting and learning from good advisors and experts in the field. I will never forget Dr. Marcie Petrini, who encouraged my sixth-grade project on comparing the acidity of soil samples from different sources around Jackson, Mississippi. Dr. Petrini taught me how to measure pH, and she showed me how much fun laboratory research could be. I thought the world of her, and she helped me see that girls could become scientists. She also taught me a lot about scientific techniques and possibilities.

In addition to science fair projects, I also became involved in science and math competitions, starting with MathCounts in the fifth grade. Our team of four competed with others from around the state in answering math questions and performing calculations quickly, as a team. I learned that speed counts, and that to make discoveries first, you have to be fast, as well as right. Working as a team to solve a problem was a new challenge. We had to answer questions quickly enough to be the first to buzz in, but we had to be right, or our team would lose the opportunity to answer a bonus question. The bonus question was solved only by all four of us working together, using our own techniques and shortcuts. Then the captain would have to make a split-second decision regarding which answer to choose for the judges. The captain had to learn to trust her teammates, for there was not time for one person to do it all (and in fact, in science, we often collaborate with people having different skills who each contribute to the research projects in a unique way). The occasional loss was devastating, but I learned from my Challenge Bowl coach, Mrs. Frances Burkett, that although you can't always win, the team will always do better next time if the team identifies the reasons that it was not successful and works on strengthening its weaknesses. This strategy has become an invaluable tool, as every mistake becomes a learning opportunity.

My first real job was as a high school assistant in a physiology and biophysics laboratory at the University of Mississippi Medical Center. This lab hires students to work after school and during the summer. The work that I did was not strictly science, though Dr. Robert Hester and his medical students did research on kidney function in hamsters. My job was to copy the new and interesting articles at the medical library and enter them into a reference database. I ached to learn more about "real science," and I would often talk to the medical students about the experiments that Dr. Hester and others were doing on renal function. He introduced me to other professors and researchers in the department, and they showed me their experiments and discussed what they hoped to discover. I did learn a bit about basic physiology, but I also learned the importance of talking to other researchers and reading the latest papers in the field that interests you.

Several times over the next few years, I did encounter people who discounted my ability to do research because of my gender, since there still are not very many women in physics. The best response to them was always simply to prove them wrong. During my freshman year in college, I was told by my math advisor not to bother competing in a national math contest because "girls can't do math." I ignored this advice and went on to do quite well on the test, beating all the other test takers from my university and proving the professor wrong. I learned not to let other people set limits on what I could achieve. A professor in physics agreed to become my official advisor, and I worked with him on scientific research that I would not have gotten involved in otherwise. This work turned out to be much more interesting! I became very interested in the work we did on chaos theory (the study of systems that depend strongly on their initial conditions), and later transferred to another university to work with an expert in the field, who had recently begun some new experiments attempting to control chaotic systems in new materials and biological systems such as the heart and certain signals in the brain. This was a good decision, for it led directly to my first scientific publication and later admission to graduate school in physics.

I love astrophysics more than anything except my husband, my family, and our dogs. I learned early on that I wanted to become a scientist or science teacher, and I did everything I could to prepare, from the science fair and MathCounts in the fifth grade to advanced classes and advanced placement tests in high school. By being prepared for tests and competitions, I was able to become a leader on projects and teams and gain confidence in my own abilities. I learned independence, discipline, teamwork, leadership, and how to use constructive criticism to make a project or presentation better the next time. I also learned that if you become good at your area of interest, no one can stand in your way.

It helps to have good female role models, but it is also important to surround yourself with smart, talented kids your age who are also interested in learning. My good friends, Adam, Cliff, Chris, Greg, Chaka, and Ian, and I worked together on math competitions, Odyssey of the Mind,

Challenge Bowl, Quiz Bowl, Mu Alpha Theta, Science Club, and countless projects for our gifted class throughout elementary, junior high, and high school. They always supported me, as I supported them, and they refused to believe any gender bias that others imposed. My friends and I dared to dream, to experiment, and to learn things beyond what we were taught, simply because it was fun. When in eighth grade we read biographies of famous scientists and each of us dressed up to speak as a scientist, my friends understood my anger when I thought my only option was Marie Curie, and they applauded more than anyone when I gave the presentation well. Having a supportive peer group helped me be confident in my abilities and learn more. I hope that you have friends like this, and that the next generation of women has their choice of female role models.

If I have any advice to give other girls, I would suggest that you find something that interests you, work to become good at it, and take every opportunity to share that interest with others. Find ways to explore related areas with other people who share your interests, both kids your age and experts in the field, perhaps at a local high school or university. Any science-related projects, teams, or activities that help you build these important skills and keep your interest in science high are important.

Find what you love, and do it well!

ALAINA JOAN OAS

ost children's playhouses are filled with delicate dishes and tiny spoons. However, in Alaina's playhouse there was a real microscope, a jar of moving grubs, a little box of snakeskins, different colors of dirt, a variety of dried plants, live earthworms, and a pet frog. Mother said only a scientist would make a laboratory out of a playhouse. A delicious mud pie filled with grubs could be made for mother at a moment's notice. Alaina's house overlooked a pond and a forest filled with animals and plants, including the twelve baby ducks she raised from eggs. Alaina spent many hours outside observing and studying the world around her. She was born Friday, November 13, 1981, in Northern Township, Minnesota. Alaina loved exploring the world around her, and always asked, "Why?" Along with winning over one hundred awards, including a research award at the International Science and Engineering Fair, Alaina's love of science and math has inspired her to receive medals, trips, certificates, and scholarship awards and has afforded her with the opportunity to meet many wonderful people.

A MUSSEL STORY

"Will this mason jar of grub worms I collected that fell off the tree be good for fishing, Dad? Let's make mother some snakeskin soup and a live grub mud pie for dessert. Let's make rose perfume out of Mother's roses." I can imagine it wasn't easy raising a little scientist. I was interested in almost everything, especially the little pond near our house. I experimented with feeding the minnows in the pond everything from peanut butter sandwiches to a salamander that disgustedly just swam away. In the backyard there were beavers, muskrats, pheasants, deer, and occasionally the neighbors' cow hungrily eating peas in our garden. I remember carrying a microscope out into the playhouse and turning it into a science laboratory when I was barely old enough to pronounce microscope. There were jars of miscellaneous leaves, bugs, and even a pet frog inhabiting my childhood playhouse. Snakes even liked to sun on the little porch there.

Who would have guessed that that little girl who collected grubs would someday be completing internationally recognized research. In fifth grade, I completed my first official science project about color and enjoyed my first taste of a science fair. In sixth grade, I researched the growth patterns of green bean plants under different colored grow lights and presented it at my second science fair. After the success of the sixth-grade project, I was able to enroll in an advanced class of thirty students doing independent research, called Project Science.

As a child, fireflies always intrigued me; therefore, my first Project Science class research was to study firefly light, called bioluminescence, under different stimuli. Four years later, I was an expert in determining time of death in pigs, cows, fish, and chickens, and could pinpoint their time of death within fifteen minutes using bioluminescence. To study time of death using bioluminescence, my back deck held decaying organs from these animals all summer. The odor of my research testing was an invitation to lunch for neighborhood animals. This caused me to build elaborate decay boxes to gently hold the decomposing tissues. Since further bioluminescence testing laboratories are rare in Minnesota, I began a research study on the native freshwater mussels of Pool 6 of the Mississippi River in eleventh grade.

A zebra mussel is a hard-shelled filter feeder that must attach to a hard surface to survive. Zebra mussels are currently attaching to native fresh-water mussels in such great numbers that the very survival of the native freshwater mussel species is threatened. One native freshwater mussel has over one thousand zebra mussels attached, making it impossible for this mussel to close its mouth or extend its foot to move or obtain food. Zebra mussels slowly kill the native freshwater mussels.

Zebra mussels are a huge economic problem for barges, locks, dams, and pipes. The only natural predators of these mussels are carp and duck; however, there are so many zebra mussels that predators cannot control their population's growth. Chlorination, different coatings, sonic vibration, high-water pressure hoses, heat, ultraviolet radiation, electric shock, chemical treatment, and bacterial controls have so far been unable to control the zebra mussel problem.

As time went on, I noticed more and more zebra mussels attaching to the shells of the native mussels of the Mississippi River. This naturally led me to question how the zebra mussels were affecting the native mussels. The bottom of the Mississippi is murky, and this makes it difficult to see. I found myself feeling on the muddy bottom of the river for the mussels I needed for research. After testing the mussels that I found, I went back and placed them exactly as I found them in the river to insure their survival. Sometimes it was difficult to even tell what was, or was not, a freshwater native mussel because of the dense zebra mussel attachment. One day I felt what I thought was a mussel and it was a zebra mussel encrusted soda can. Even a brick tricked me into thinking it was a mussel, but wasn't, because it was so covered with zebra mussels.

The Mississippi River in Winona is a beautiful sight with the bluffs in the background and the islands in the river. Yet, when you get involved with the river, there are the usual bugs like mosquitoes, chiggers, and even leaches. The water in the Mississippi River is cool even in the summer, so it is easy to forget sunscreen when you are cold. After that first massive sunburn, I never forgot again. Another problem was the fast currents, so great care had to be taken not to be carried away. A diver's flag was used so larger boats of the Mississippi River would give me the space I needed. Some zipped on by, but many stopped to chat and look at my work and all the samples that I had collected that day. There were even some people asking me, "What is a zebra mussel?"

Statistically, I determined zebra mussels were attaching near the feeding inhalant siphon of the native mussel. This means they could be taking the native mussels' food away. To do this research, I first invented a location code to determine where zebra mussels were attaching on the native mussels. My second invention was a size class chart for the zebra mussels to determine what size class was attaching. My third was a roughness index to determine on which type of surface the zebra mussels preferred to attach. This research has won over forty awards through the local, regional, state, and international science fairs.

After studying my research results, I decided to continue this research in twelfth grade by studying the feeding patterns of zebra mussels versus native mussels. To do this, I set up twelve aquariums, each containing different ratios of zebra mussels to native mussels. After twenty-six weeks of study and thousands of growth measurements, it was determined that zebra mussels were drastically taking away the native mussels' food supply when the ratio of zebra mussels to native mussels was greater than one to one.

In my quest for mussels, sometimes I worried about my little boat being able to cross the fast moving currents of the Mississippi River to Pool 6. It took some time but I made it. Some youngsters stole this same little boat, with a patched hole in the bottom, during my research. Fortunately, they were unwise enough to put it in their yard where I spotted it while canoeing. The police recovered it just in time to continue and finish my research.

As a young student in Project Science, I always dreamed of two goals in order to reach the pinnacle of independent research for my age. These goals were to compete in the prestigious Intel International Science and Engineering Fair and the Tri-State Junior Science and Humanities Symposium. I did both in eleventh grade. In May 1999, I reached my first goal, which was to take my mussel research to the international fair and win a coveted grand award. Everyone who participates in this event dreams of such a moment. In addition, I won first place in the world from the North American Benthological Society and was invited to present my research at their annual international meeting. The Benthological Society is composed of researchers studying river life from all over the world.

In twelfth grade, I surpassed any goal I had previously set. I advanced to the 2000 Intel International Science and Engineering Fair held in Detroit, Michigan, to compete with my research on mussel growth patterns. I competed with people from all over the world with their research from places like China, Japan, Canada, and Venezuela. It was fun to meet people from all over the world with scientific interests similar to mine. Several Nobel Prize winners attended and talked with competitors about their projects. I was fortunate to be able to talk with the Nobel Prize winners. After an intense session of judging, my research won first place in the world. It also won recognition from the Department of the Interior. I was very proud of this accomplishment because along with a scholarship prize, my first place win also provided a thousand dollars each for my school and the science fair.

My second goal was reached in October 1999 when I won the Tri-State Junior Science and Humanities Symposium. Competitors were students from Minnesota, North Dakota, and South Dakota. In April, I was able to represent Minnesota, North Dakota, and South Dakota in the National Science and Humanities Symposium held in Washington, D.C. This exciting competition represents the top research paper competition in the nation. At this competition, my research paper won third place in the United States and territories. I will never forget when an army general presented me with a medal, certificate, and scholarship.

The people I have met during my research have been my role models. My first role models were my Project Science teachers, Jerry and Judee Foster. My malacological advisor, Marian Havlik, provided further professional advice and encouragement. Listening to role models and asking questions was very important in the process of learning and discovering.

Sometimes when I go to elementary schools to teach young students about science, they ask me how I had the courage and persistence to reach this level of competition. I tell them to set their goals high, work hard, and to not be afraid of trying something new. Even if everything doesn't work as intended, be proud of your success in trying. Every question is important, and even if something doesn't work, at least you have discovered what not to do. Winning is the icing on the cake, but the real award is the knowledge and experience gained through our endeavors.

In closing, be curious, ask questions, try new things, listen, and enjoy the people and the world around you. Especially, explore the world of books because they can take you to any time, place, or person you wish to meet. I have always enjoyed reading books by Lloyd C. Douglas, Lord Byron, and William Durant. Since each of the authors wrote about Roman and Greek civilization, I decided to learn Latin and Greek, which is very useful in studying science. It doesn't hurt to have parents who will let you turn your little playhouse into a science laboratory. My parents allowed me to be curious about my world, even if initially it was collecting grubs to put in a mason jar. In this way I became an active participant in my world. I think children today need the time to explore and enjoy our world wherever they may live.

YING

WU

Ying was born in Nanjing, China, July 22, 1977. At the age of seven, she left China and arrived in New York City, where she has lived ever since. Children pick up new languages very quickly, so Ying could speak English fluently after one year in the United States. As a young child, Ying spent most of her free time reading detective novels like the Nancy Drew series. Ying's parents, who are physicists, and her high school, Stuyvesant High School, heavily emphasized the importance of science. When her father was ill, she became very interested in medicine so that she could one day make him feel better. From high school, she was accepted into a dual bachelor of arts and medical degree program at New York University, which meant that she had a reserved spot at NYU medical school after college.

LOVE OF RESEARCH

In college, I took many science courses because of my premedical track and my biology major. During my sophomore year, I started to conduct research in biochemistry. Since many doctors conduct research, I thought that it was a good idea to get some scientific experience as soon as possible.

My research proposal received a Dean's Undergraduate Research Fund that could pay for equipment and other supplies. The purpose of the project was to determine whether unusual chemical bonds, called cross-links, are formed between protein and DNA (genetic information found in human cells in the form of strands of molecules) by reactive particles. In human cells, DNA and protein are often in close contact. Any cross-links between them are harmful to cells because they block the normal function of DNA, and thus can lead to cancer, the unregulated growth of cells. The reactive particles that cause formation of cross-links are generated by special light-sensitive molecules such as benzopyrene diol epoxide (BPDE). BPDE can be formed in the body as a result of eating grilled food, breathing in exhaust fumes from cars, and so on. When strong light, such as sunlight, shines upon a human cell that contains BPDE, reactive particles are generated and can travel from one location in a DNA strand to another. My research project used double-stranded DNA with one strand longer than the other. BPDE was attached to the shorter strand of DNA. A special protein called single strand binding protein (SSB) that is commonly associated with DNA in cells was attached to the longer strand of DNA at some distance from the BPDE. The DNA-SSB-BPDE complexes were exposed to a strong light (similar to sunlight), a process called irradiation, for different lengths of time. Because of the irradiation, the light-sensitive BPDE produced reactive particles. A chemical technique called denaturing gel electrophoresis, which allows one to distinguish between different molecules on the basis of their size, was used to determine whether cross-links were formed. Cross-linked DNA-SSB were larger in size. The results confirmed the hypothesis that the strong light, after a minimum period of irradiation, produced reactive particles from BPDE. These reactive particles then caused unusual DNA-protein cross-links that are lethal to a cell. The amount of cross-links formed increased with irradiation time, but only up to a certain point, after which increased irradiation did not increase cross-link formation. The explanation for this will be sought in future research that will investigate the exact mechanism of cross-link formation itself.

Research is very interesting because it gives me the chance to discover new things about nature. Like the detective novels I loved to read as a child, research calls for answering questions through hands-on investigation, collection of data, and interpretation of the clues (data). I have the chance to discover something that will benefit humankind. Research is also an application of theories learned in the classroom, which enlivens classroom learning.

Certainly research was intimidating at first, but many undergraduate students at my university conduct research, so I thought to myself that I could handle it, too. The lab was filled with unfamiliar equipment, and people talked using words that weren't even on the SAT. The articles I was asked to read seemed to be written in a Martian tongue. However, things improved quickly. After taking more advanced science classes, like molecular cell biology, all of the unfamiliar vocabulary and the theory behind the experimental techniques became clear. Now, I can talk like a biologist and understand other biologists with no trouble. Scientific articles that I once dreaded reading are now very interesting. The graduate students in the lab trained me to use the equipment, and I can now design and conduct my own experiments. It's a rewarding feeling of accomplishment.

Conducting research is a great learning experience. I have to think creatively to design experiments and analytically to evaluate the data collected in order to draw conclusions from the experiments. To design experiments and to interpret data, I must have a thorough mastery of biochemistry. This mastery certainly takes much time and dedication, and involves studying when my friends are at the movies, but the rewards of research and the understanding of a subject make the work well worth it. I still remember how exciting it was to be able to run my first polyacrylamide gel without any assistance. I even took a picture of the gel as a memento to remind me of the progress I had made.

Recently, I presented my research at the Undergraduate Research Conference. The judges and professors told me that I had a thorough understanding of my research, and that was very gratifying. Sure, I've had to stay late at night in the laboratory and had to sacrifice a few social events, but I would definitely do it all over again. Research nurtures skills of critical and creative thinking that are invaluable in life.

My primary female role model is my mother, who is herself a scientist. My aunts and female cousins are also scientists, so they, too, serve as role models for me. In my family, both females and males are expected to be intelligent, capable, and educated.

Anyone who likes science should definitely pursue research. Do not be intimidated by the complex vocabulary, experiments, or equipment. You will slowly but surely master anything that puzzles you at first.

Part III

ADDITIONAL

INSPIRATION

THE ACCOMPLISHMENTS
OF WOMEN

in Science,
Mathematics,
and Technology

W omen have always been leaders in these fields. Perhaps there are some who you will recognize and a few who will be new to you. As you read these impressive timelines of accomplishments, add to them from your readings and thoughts over the coming decades. Put a date on this listing when you have or will be recognized for your outstanding work in one of these fields. An inspirational activity would be for you and/or your female friends to develop a timeline of girls in your school and/or community who have made accomplishments in these areas.

Much of the information used to generate the timelines in this section was gathered from Web sites and resource books pertaining to women in science, mathematics, and technology. Some very useful resources for biographies of prominent women in these fields include:

Contributions of 20th Century Women to Physics
    http://www.physics.ucla.edu/~cwp

Women Inventors
    http://www.inventorsmuseum.com/women.htm

Nobel Prize Internet Archive
    http://www.almaz.com/nobel/nobel.htm

4000 Years of Women in Science
    http://www.astr.ua.edu/4000WS/4000WS.html

Biographies of Women Mathematicians
    http://www.agnesscott.edu/lriddle/women/women.htm

Past Notable Women in Mathematics
    http://www.cs.yale.edu/homes/tap/past-women-math.html

Past Notable Women in Computing
    http://www.cs.yale.edu/homes/tap/past-women-cs.html

Check out the resource section at the end of this book for other ideas!

WOMEN IN SCIENCE

Ancient China

Shi Dun   China   Inventor
Developed the first paper from the bark of mulberry trees.

Ancient Greece

Aglaonike   Greece   Natural Philosopher
First female astronomer who learned the phases of the moon and "predicted" lunar eclipses.

Circa first century

Mary Hebraea   Egypt   Alchemist
Discovered the formula for hydrochloric acid.

1099–1179

Hildegard von Bingen   Germany   Mystic, Scholar
Correctly theorized the concept of universal gravitation centuries before Isaac Newton.

1600s

Martine de Beausoleil   France   Geologist
Wrote about the discovery of valuable ores and their importance to the European economy which resulted in the King of France becoming one of the wealthiest rulers in all of Europe.

1670–1720

Maria Margarethe Kirch   Germany   Astronomer
Discovered the comet of 1702.

1750–1848

Caroline Herschel   Germany   Astronomer
Discovered eight comets and three nebulas. She received the gold medal of the Royal Astronomical Society.

1794–1871

Jeanne Villepreux-Power   France   Marine Biologist
First to create and use aquariums for experimentation in aquatic environments. Known as the "mother" of aquariophily.

1799–1847

Mary Anning   England   Fossil Collector
First female paleontologist.

1808–?

Caterina Scarpellini   Italy   Astronomer
Organized the Meteorological Ozonometric station in Rome. She discovered a comet in 1854, and in 1872 was awarded a gold medal by the new government in Italy for her work in statistics.

1818–1889

Maria Mitchell   USA   Astronomer
Discovered a new comet. She was the first woman to be elected to the American Academy of Arts and Sciences.

1820–1910

Florence Nightingale   England   Nurse
Known as the "lady with the lamp" because she cared for patients around the clock and demanded supplies and better hospital conditions, her undying dedication helped shape nursing into the profession it is today.

1821–1910

Elizabeth Blackwell   England   Physician
America's first female doctor.

1826–1910

Emily Blackwell   England   Physician
Ran the New York Infirmary for Women and Children and the Women's Medical College and provided training for women in medicine. She was also Elizabeth Blackwell's younger sister.

1832–1919

Mary Edwards Walker   USA   Physician
Known as a "bloomerite" who dressed in men's clothes as she practiced medicine, she was the only woman from the Civil War to receive the Congressional Medal of Honor. Her name appears on a plaque in the Pentagon.

1839–1917

Elizabeth Garrett Anderson   England   Physician
First British female physician, she established a clinic for women and children in London, which is now named after her.

1840–1912

Sophia Louisa Jex-Blake   England   Physician
Fought for the right for women to earn medical degrees.

1842–1911

Ellen Henrietta Swallow Richards USA   Chemist, Engineer
First woman elected to the American Institute of Mining and Metallurgical Engineers. Originator of the terms ecology *and* euthenics.

1847–1920

Mary Watson Whitney   USA   Astronomer
Trained the first generation of highly educated female astronomers.

1848–1915

Margaret Lindsey Murray Huggins   Ireland   Astronomer
Codiscovered the Orion nebula.

1854–1923

Hertha Ayrton   England   Physicist, Engineer
One of the first female electrical engineers, she improved the working of the electric arc, used in lighting of her time.

1857–1945

Ida Henrietta Hyde   USA   Physiologist
Developed the microelectrode. First female member of the American Physiological Society and first woman to conduct research at Harvard Medical School.

1859–1953

Alice Eastwood   USA   Botanist
Collected rare botanical specimens for the California Academy of Sciences in San Francisco.

1861–1912

Nettie Stevens   USA   Research Biologist
Discovered the X and Y chromosomes that determine the sex of humans.

1862–1945

Florence Bascom   USA   Geologist
First female vice president for the Geological Society of America.

1863–1941

Annie Jump Cannon   USA   Astronomer
Observed and cataloged over 350,000 stars while working at the Harvard Observatory.

1867–1934

Marie Curie   Poland/France   Radiochemist
Discovered radioactive elements, and codiscovered polonium and radium. Awarded Nobel Prize in physics in 1903 and 1911.

1867–1953

Ida Gray   USA   Dentist
First African American woman to earn the doctor of dental surgery degree in the United States. She was also the first African American woman to practice dentistry in Chicago.

1869–1970

Alice Hamilton   USA   Physician, Pathologist
Founder of occupational medicine who specialized in industrial diseases. Her efforts helped pave the way for forced occupational safety.

1870–1952

Maria Montessori   Italy   Physician
First woman in Italy to become a doctor of medicine. She developed a system of education for children that teaches freedom and responsibility. She later founded the Montessori school.

1871–1953

Florence Rena Sabin   USA   Physiologist

First female president of the American Association of Anatomists and recipient of the Lasker Award, the highest honor given in the medical profession. She is responsible for the implementation of mammograms for women.

1876–1954

Edith Patch Marion   USA   Entomologist

International expert on aphids.

1881–1975

Alice Evans   USA   Microbiologist

Discovered the organism that caused undulant fever in cows. This resulted in mandatory milk pasteurization, which saved lives worldwide.

1878–1898

Lilian Moller Gilbreth   USA   Industrial Engineer

Pioneer in the field of time-and-motion studies.

1878–1968

Lise Meitner   Austria   Theoretical Physicist

First identified nuclear fission.   /Sweden

1880–1972

Emma Perry Carr   USA   Physical Chemist

Studied physical chemistry.

1883–1974

Margaret Morse Nice   USA   Ornithologist

Combined knowledge of birds, psychology, and language to advance the study of bird behavior.

1887–1948

Ruth Benedict   USA   Anthropologist

An important figure in cultural anthropology, her research greatly contributed to the field and to the theory of cultural relativity. One of the first female anthropologists of her time.

1887–1972

Louise Arner Boyd   USA   Explorer

Arctic explorer and the first woman to fly over the North Pole.

1889–1971

Emma Lucy Braun   USA   Botanist, Ecologist

First female president of the Ecological Society of America. Her dedication and efforts to land preservation instigated the introduction of plant ecology as an academic discipline.

1897–1956

Irène Joliot-Curie   France   Physicist, Chemist

Daughter of Physicist Marie Curie. She and her husband, Fredric Joliot, won the Noble Prize in chemistry in 1935 for creating new radioactive elements.

1896–1957

Gerty Radnitz Cori   Czechoslovakia   Biochemist
                                     /USA
Became first American woman to receive the Nobel Prize, when her husband and she were awarded the Nobel Prize in medicine in 1947.

1897–1967

Tilly Edinger   Germany   Paleontologist
Founder of paleoneurology.

1897–1991

Florence Selbert   USA   Scientist
Involved in cancer research. Made it possible to test for Tuberculosis.

1898–1937

Amelia Earhart   USA   Aviator
First woman to fly across the Atlantic Ocean alone, establishing a new record for the crossing: 13 hrs 30 min. Best known for her attempt to fly around the world in 1937. Her disappearance still remains a mystery.

1900–1979

Cecelia Payne-Gaposchkin   England   Astronomer
First to receive a Ph.D. in astronomy from the Harvard College Observatory, she also was the first woman to head the university's astronomy department.

1901–1978

Margaret Mead   USA   Anthropologist
Widely known for her studies of primitive societies.

1902–1992

Barbara McClintock   USA   Geneticist
Developed the theory of transposition within chromosomes.

1903–1974

Irmgard Flügge-Lotz   Germany   Engineer
Stanford's first female professor of engineering, she made improvements in the design of aircraft with the introduction of automatic controls, which made jet aircraft possible.

1905–1993

Helen Sawyer Hogg   USA/Canada Astronomer
Codiscovered variable stars.

1906–1980

Col. Jacqueline Cochran   USA   Aviator
First American female aviator to break the sound barrier and to pilot a bomber across the Atlantic Ocean. She also directed the Women's Air Force Service Pilots during WWII.

1906–1972

Maria Goeppart Mayer   Germany   Theoretical Physicist
Investigated the nucleus of the atom which earned her the Nobel Prize in physics in 1963.

1906–1976

Sarah Stewart   Mexico   Biologist
Codiscovered the SE Polyoma Virus.

1907–1964

Rachel Carson   USA   Zoologist,
                                              Environmentalist
Credited for awakening America's ecological conscience and launching today's environmental movement, through her publications.

1907–1977

Dorothy Hill   Australia   Geologist,
                                              Paleontologist
Played a major role in establishing the field of paleontology in Australia. She was a world authority on fossil corals.

1908–1977

Myra Adele Logan   USA   Physician
First African American woman to be elected as a member of the American College of Surgeons and the first woman in the world to perform open-heart surgery. She is considered to be a pioneer for African American women's rights.

1909–

Rita Levi-Montalcini   Italy   Biologist
Major contributor to the understanding of growth factors. Received the Nobel Prize in medicine in 1986.

1910–1994

Dorothy Crowfoot Hodgkin   Egypt   Physical Chemist
Awarded the Nobel Prize for chemistry in 1964 for determining x-ray techniques of the structure of biologically important molecules. Discovered the structures of penicillin and vitamin B-12.

1912–1997

Chien-Shiung Wu   China   Theoretical Physicist
Studied beta radiation.

1913–1998

Mary Nichol Leaky   England   Anthropologist
Codiscovered skulls of Australopithecines and Homo habilus, some of the earliest possible ancestors of man.

1913–1994

Effie O'Neal Ellis   USA   Physician
First African American administrator in the American Medical Association. She was a specialist in maternal, prenatal, postnatal, and preventative health care.

1917–

Irene Ayako Uchida   Canada   Biologist
Down syndrome researcher.

1918–1999

Gertrude Belle Elion   USA   Biochemist
Received forty-five patents on medicines for leukemia, herpes, malaria, gout, AIDS, and antirejection drugs for organ transplants.

1920–1958

Rosalind Elsie Franklin   England   Molecular Biologist
Responsible for much of the research and discovery work that led to the understanding of the structure of DNA.

1920–

Katherine Siva Saubel   USA   Ethnoanthropologist
Native American who was determined to preserve her tribe's culture and language. Founder of the Malki Museum, which was the first to be founded and run by Native Americans.

1921–

Rosalyn Sussman Yalow   USA   Nuclear Physicist
First woman to receive the Albert Laster Award, in 1976, she became the second woman to receive the Nobel Prize for medicine, in 1977. Together with Dr. Sol Bernson, she discovered how to measure small amounts of hormones in the human body by using radioisotopes.

1923–

Joanne Simpson   USA   Meteorology
First woman to earn a Ph.D. in meteorology.

1924–

Jewel Plummer Cobb   USA   Cell Biologist
Made important discoveries about how cells grow, divide, and become cancerous. Also known for promoting minority involvement in the sciences.

1926–

R. Rajalakshmi   India   Biochemist, Nutritionist
Developed recipes and educational programs that greatly improved the diets, health, and lives of India's people.

1928–

Vera Rubin   USA   Astronomer

A pioneer in the study of the motions of galaxies and dark matter and also the first woman "permitted" to observe at the Palomar Observatory, she was awarded the National Medal of Science in 1993.

1932–1985

Dian Fossey   USA   Zoologist,
                                           Environmentalist

Best known for her research with the mountain gorilla.

1934–

Jane Goodall   England   Ethologist

Best known for her studies of chimpanzees, her research broadened the scientific study and thought regarding human evolution.

1934–

Julia Levy   Canada   Immunologist

Codiscoverer of photosensitizer anticancer drugs, a treatment that combines drugs and light.

1935–

Sylvia Earle   USA   Marine Biologist

Lived underwater for two weeks as part of the NASA-sponsored project called Tektite. She has also dived deeper than any other solo diver.

1937–

Valentina Tereshkova   Russia   Cosmonaut

First woman in space.

1943–

Shannon Lucid   USA   Biochemist, Astronaut
The only woman to receive the Congressional Space Medal of Honor, she holds the record for the most flight hours in orbit by any woman in the world.

1943–

Jocelyn Bell Burnell   Ireland   Astronomer
Discovered the first four pulsars.

1944–

Antonia Coello Novello   Puerto Rico/USA   Pediatrician
First Hispanic woman to hold the position of the United States Surgeon General.

1948–

Svetlana Savitskaya   Russia   Astronaut
Became the second woman in space, in 1982.

1948–1986

Sharon C. McAuliffe   USA   Educator
Was chosen by NASA to participate in the Teacher in Space Project aboard the Challenger spacecraft but was tragically killed when the Challenger exploded seventy-eight seconds after take-off. She is still known as the first teacher in space.

1949–1986

Judith Resnik   USA   Engineer, Astronaut
Joined NASA in 1978 as one of the first six women ever accepted to the U.S. Space Program. On January 26, 1986, she was aboard the Challenger spacecraft, which exploded shortly after take-off. She would have specialized in testing equipment and doing experiments in orbit.

1951–

| Sally Kristen Ride | USA | Astrophysicist |

First American female astronaut.

1956–

| Mae C. Jemison | USA | Biomedical Engineer, Physician, Astronaut |

First African American astronaut.

1956–

| Col. Eileen M. Collins | USA | Astronaut |

First woman to command a mission in space.

1958–

| Ellen Ochoa | USA | Astronaut |

First Hispanic American astronaut.

WOMEN IN MATHEMATICS

5th Century B.C.E.

Theano   Greece   Mathematician
Theano and her two daughters carried on the Pythagorean School after the death of Pythagoras, her husband. She wrote treatises on mathematics, physics, medicine, and child psychology. Her most important work was the principle of the "Golden Mean."

Ca. 370–414

Hypatia   Egypt   Mathematician
Edited the work On the Conics of Apollonius, *which divided cones into different parts by a plane. With her work on this important book, she made the concepts easier to understand, thus making the work survive through many centuries. She was the first woman to have such a profound impact on the survival of early thought in mathematics.*

1646–1684

Elena Lucrezia Cornaro Piscopia   Italy   Mathematician
Became a mathematics lecturer at the University of Padua in 1678. Her writings were published in 1688 in Parma, Italy, after her death. Even today she is widely quoted by other scholars and writers.

1706–1749

Emilie du Chatelet   France   Mathematician
Explained one part of Leibniz's system in Institutions de Physique. *She was extremely successful in translating Newton's book on the principals of mathematics into French. She also added to this book an "Algebraical Commentary" which very few general readers understood.*

1718–1799

Maria Gaetana Agnesi   Italy   Mathematician

Best known for the curve called the "Witch of Agnesi," her book, Analytical Institutions, *was one of the first and most complete works on finite and infinitesimal analysis. This book became a model of clarity and was widely translated and used as a textbook.*

1776–1831

Sophie Germain   France   Mathematician

A revolutionary who became a celebrated mathematician despite gender prejudices and her lack of formal education, she is best known for her work in number theory, but her work in the theory of elasticity is also very important to mathematics.

1780–1872

Mary Fairfax Somerville   Scotland   Mathematician,
                                                   Astronomer

Her book, Physical Geography, *was widely used in schools and universities for over fifty years.*

1815–1852

Ada Byron Lovelace   England   Mathematician

Encouraged by her mother to pursue mathematics and not to become a poet like her father, Lord Byron, she was interested in "computing machines," and predicted their vast applications over a century before the invention of the computer. In 1979, the U.S. government dedicated a software language in her name.

1832–1916

Mary Everest Boole   England   Mathematician

Considered by herself a mathematical psychologist because of her dedication to understanding how children learned mathematics, she published many books on this topic, and her contributions are used in modern classrooms today.

1842–1921

Susan Jane Cunningham   USA   Mathematician,
                                                Astronomer

Assisted in starting the astronomy and mathematics departments for Swarthmore College. She headed the departments until her retirement 1906, during which time she was promoted to full professor.

1845–1919

Elizaveta Fedorovna Litvinova   Russia   Mathematician

Published over seventy articles on the philosophy and practice of teaching mathematics. Respected as one of the foremost pedagogues in Russia.

1847–1930

Christine Ladd-Franklin   USA   Mathematician,
                                                Psychologist

Active advocate of graduate education and academic employment for women. Her main focus in mathematics was symbolic logic. She is well known for her dissertation, The Algebra of Logic.

1850–1891

Sofya Kovalevskaya   Russia   Mathematician

Referred to as the "Princess of Science" because she was a distinguished professor of mathematics at the University of Stockholm.

1851–1930

Ellen Amanda Hayes   USA   Mathematician

One of the first six women to join the New York Mathematical Society, which later became the American Mathematical Society.

1854–1923

Hertha Ayrton   England   Mathematician,
                                            Engineer

Invented a draftsman's device that could be used for dividing up a line into equal parts as well as for enlarging and reducing figures. She was elected the first female member of the Institution of Electrical Engineers, and was also the first woman to ever read her own paper before the Royal Society of London.

1858–1931

Charlotte Agnas Scott   England   Mathematician

Considered to be a pioneer for the advancement of women's role in the field of mathematics, she was the first British woman to receive a doctorate in mathematics and was the first mathematician at Bryn Mawr College.

1860–1934

Charlotte Barnum   USA   Mathematician

Became the first of three women to receive a Ph.D. in mathematics from Yale before 1900.

1860–1940

Alicia Boole Stott   Ireland   Mathematician

The third of the five daughters of Mary Everest Boole. Although she never received formal education in mathematics, she still was very well versed in geometry. She remained interested in regular and semiregular four-dimensional polytopes and made several important discoveries in this area.

1862–1917

Ruth Gentry   USA   Mathematician

Taught at Vassar College from 1896 until 1902, where she was the first mathematics faculty member to hold a Ph.D.

1862–1951

Winifred Edgerton Merrill   USA   Mathematician
The first American woman to receive a Ph.D. in mathematics, in 1906 she founded the Oaksmere School for Girls, which she directed until 1928. It became well known for its high scholastic standards.

1866–1948

Clara Latimer Bacon   USA   Mathematician
Became the first woman to receive a Ph.D. in mathematics from Johns Hopkins University.

1868–1944

Grace Chisholm Young   England/Germany   Mathematician
The first woman to officially receive a doctorate in any field in Germany. Besides her extensive work in mathematics, she also completed all the requirements for a medical degree except the internship, learned six languages, and taught each of her six children a musical instrument.

1869–1959

Mary Frances Winston Newson   USA   Mathematician
First American woman to receive a Ph.D. in mathematics from a European university.

1870–1917

Agnes Baxter   Canada   Mathematician
Fourth woman to receive a Ph.D. in mathematics in North America and the second Canadian woman to do so.

1870–1945

Virginia Ragsdale   USA   Mathematician

Formulated the Ragsdale Conjecture, which was an important open problem in the field of real algebraic geometry. It was researched for over ninety years and a correct upper-bound to replace it is still unknown.

1871–?

Roxana Hayward Vivian   USA   Mathematician

Became the first woman to receive a Ph.D. in mathematics from the University of Pennsylvania.

1872–1965

Elizabeth Street Dickerman   USA   Mathematician

Second woman to receive a Ph.D. in mathematics from Yale University. She was also a poet and a writer.

1875–1962

Grace Marie Bareis   USA   Mathematician

First woman to receive a Ph.D. in mathematics from Ohio State University.

1881–1967

Mayme I. Logsdon   USA   Mathematician

Only woman to hold a regular faculty position at the University of Chicago above the rank of instructor before 1982.

1882–1935

Emmy Noether   Germany   Mathematician

Teacher whose pacifistic teaching style encouraged students to teach themselves and become successful. She spent most of her time studying abstract algebra and had the ability to examine complex algebraical relationships as others could not.

1883–1966

Anna Pell Wheeler   USA   Mathematician
First woman to give the Colloquium Lectures at the American Mathematical Society meetings.

1885–1940

Annie Dale Biddle Andrews   USA   Mathematician
First woman to receive a Ph.D. in mathematics from the University of California at Berkeley.

1885–1967

Pauline Sperry   USA   Mathematician
First woman promoted to assistant professor in the mathematics department at Berkeley. She specialized in geometry, and the "Sperry's Curve" was named after her.

1890–1974

Olive Clio Hazlett   USA   Mathematician
Wrote more professional papers than any other pre-1940 American female mathematician.

1894–1974

Cecilia Krieger   Poland   Mathematician
First European woman, and the third person overall, to earn a Ph.D. in mathematics from a Canadian University.

1896–1966

Sof'ja Aleksandrovna Janovskaja   Russia   Mathematician
First chairperson of the Department of Mathematical Logic at Moscow State University.

1898–1988

Marguerite Lehr   USA   Mathematician
Conducted a highly successful series of television mathematics classes on a Philadelphia TV program called University of the Air *1953–54.*

1898–1996

Gertrude Blanch   Poland   Mathematician
Pioneer in numerical analysis and computation. She published over thirty papers on functional approximation, numerical analysis, and Mathieu functions.

1899–?

Pelageya Yakovlevna   Russia   Mathematician
  Polubarinova-Kochina
One of the most important female mathematicians and scientists in the Soviet Union, she was instrumental in the establishment and direction of various academic departments in hydromechanics and hydrodynamics during her time.

1900–1978

Gertrude Mary Cox   USA   Mathematician
Founder of the Department of Experimental Statistics at North Carolina State University, the Institute of Statistics of the Consolidated University of North Carolina, and the Statistics Research Division of the Research Triangle Institute. In 1949, she became the first female elected into the International Statistical Institute.

1900–1998

Mary Lucy Cartwright   England   Mathematician
First female mathematician to be elected as a Fellow of the Royal Society of England. She was elected President of the London Mathematical Society in 1951 and in 1969 became Dame Mary Cartwright (the female equivalent of a knighthood).

1901–1961

Nina Karlovna Bari   Russia   Mathematician

First woman to present her principal conclusions on trigonometric series to the Moscow Mathematical Society. She was also the first female student at Moscow State University.

1902–1997

Mina Rees   USA   Mathematician

First female president of the American Association for the Advancement of Science.

1903–1974

Irmgard Flügge-Lotz   Germany   Engineer,
                                        Mathematician

Internationally renowned for her contributions to aerodynamics and automatic theory control, she was Stanford's first female professor of engineering.

1905–1977

Rózsa Péter   Hungary   Mathematician

Helped to found the modern field of recursive function theory as a separate area of mathematical research. In 1952, she was the first Hungarian female mathematician to become an Academic Doctor of Mathematics.

1905–1977

Ruth Moufang   Germany   Mathematician

First woman in Germany to be appointed as a full professor at the University of Frankfurt, in 1957. She assisted in creating a new mathematical specialty in the algebraic analysis of projective planes that drew upon a mixture of geometry and algebra.

1906–1995

Olga Taussky-Todd   Czechoslovakia   Mathematician
First woman to teach at California Institute of Technology under a formal appointment and the first woman to be named full professor there.

1907–1963

Margaret Jarman Hagood   USA   Mathematician
Made significant contributions to the application of statistics to sociological research.

1909–1993

Florence Nightingale David   USA   Mathematician
Known for her efforts in opening the door to women in statistics.

1912–1981

Cora Ratto de Sadosky   Argentina   Mathematician
Part of the team that built a modern School of Sciences at the University of Buenos Aires, she was instrumental in the organization of advanced courses for several generations of mathematicians and scientists.

1914–1971

Hanna Neumann   Australia   Mathematician
Became the head of the Department of Pure Mathematics in the National University's School of General Studies in Australia. She was also one of the founding vice presidents of the Australian Association of Mathematics Teachers in 1966.

1914–1979

Marjorie Lee Browne   USA   Mathematician
Earned her doctorate from the University of Michigan in 1949 and was one of the first two African American women to earn a doctorate in mathematics. She chaired the Mathematics Department at North Carolina College 1951–1970, and in 1975 was the first recipient of the W.W. Rankin Memorial Award for Excellence in Mathematics Education, given by the North Carolina Council of Teachers of Mathematics. During the last years of her life, Dr. Browne helped finance gifted math students' pursuit of their education.

1914–1988

Dorothy Lewis Bernstein   USA   Mathematician
First female president of the Mathematical Association of America 1979–1980.

1915–

Alice T. Schafer   USA   Mathematician
One of the founding members of the Association for Women in Mathematics in 1971 and president 1973–75. In 1990 the Association for Women in Mathematics established the Alice T. Schafer Mathematics Prize to honor her for her many years of unselfish and dedicated service toward increasing the participation of women in mathematics.

1917–

Ruth Aaronson Bari   USA   Mathematician
Recognized for her influential work in graph theory, especially in the area of chromatic polynomials.

1919–1985

Julia Robinson   USA   Mathematician
First woman elected to membership in the National Academy of Sciences. She is best known for her important contributions to number theory.

1923–

Yvonne Choquet-Bruhat   France   Mathematician
First woman elected to the French Academy of Sciences in its three hundred-year history. She was also elected to the American Academy of Arts and Sciences in 1985.

1923–

Cathleen Morawetz   Canada   Mathematician
First woman in the United States to head a mathematical institute when she was named director of the Courant Institute of Mathematical Sciences in 1984. In 1995, she became only the second woman to be elected as president of the American Mathematical Society in the Society's 105-year history. She is now professor emeritus at New York University-Courant Institute.

1932–1989

Louise Hay   France   Mathematician
Appointed as head of the Department of Mathematics at the University of Illinois at Chicago in 1980. At that time she was the only female head of a major research-oriented university mathematics department in the United States.

1932–1995

Vivienne Malone-Mayes   USA   Mathematician
First African American to earn a Ph.D. in mathematics from the University of Texas. She was also the first African American faculty member at Baylor University, man or woman.

1933–

Etta Falconer   USA   Mathematician
A founder of the National Association of Mathematicians, an organization that promotes concerns of black students and mathematicians.

1935–

Alexandra Bellow   Romania   Mathematician

Received her Ph.D. from Yale in 1959 and works in the area of ergodic theory. Dr. Bellow has been a full professor at Northwestern University since 1968.

1935–

Gloria Hewitt   USA   Mathematician

Third African American woman to earn a Ph.D. in mathematics.

1935–

Bhama Srinivasan   India   Mathematician

Former president of the Association for Women in Mathematics. She researches the representation theory of finite groups.

1936–

Argelia Velez-Rodriguez   Cuba   Mathematician

First minority woman to receive a doctorate from the University of Havana in 1960. She also became the program manager with the Minority Institutions Science Improvement Program in Washington, D.C., and has been a program director for the Department of Education since 1980.

1939–

Mary Gray   USA   Mathematician

One of the primary founders of the Association for Women in Mathematics and its first president from 1971 to 1973. In 1976, she was elected the second female vice president of the American Mathematical Society.

1939–

Doris Schattschneider   USA   Mathematician

Instrumental in opening the world of visual geometry to others, her dual interest in geometry and art led her to study the work of Dutch artist M.C. Escher and its relationship to math.

1940–

Linda Keen   USA   Mathematician

Former president of the Association for Women in Mathematics and vice president of the American Mathematical Society.

1942–

Nancy Kopell   USA   Mathematician

First woman to become the C. L. E. Moore Instructor of Mathematics at MIT. She is particularly interested in studying the relationship between biology and math.

1942–

Karen Uhlenbeck   USA   Mathematician

One of the few mathematicians acknowledged as an expert in theoretical physics.

1943–

Lenore Blum   USA   Mathematician

First woman editor of the International Journal of Algebra and Computation. *Instrumental in increasing the participation of women and girls in mathematics. She has conducted research to study why some problems are hard for computers to solve.*

1944–

Krystyna Kuperberg   Poland   Mathematician

Specializes in the study of topology and discrete geometry. In 1987, she solved an old problem of Knaster concerning bihomogeneity of continua.

1944–

Jean Taylor   USA   Mathematician
Has engaged in interesting studies of soap bubbles, crystals, and other "minimal surfaces." Her work has been published in the Annals of Mathematics.

1945–

Dusa McDuff   Scotland   Mathematician
Internationally known geometer, specializing in symplectic geometry.

1945–

Linda Rothschild   USA   Mathematician
Writes algorithms for factoring polynomials over the integers. She has established a scholarship for talented junior high school girls to accelerate their mathematical training by participating in a summer program.

1949–

Fan Chung   Taiwan   Mathematician
Interested in the study of combinatorics, a bridge between mathematics and computer science.

1954–

Ingrid Daubechies   Belgium   Mathematician
Internationally recognized for her work in Weyl quantization, a mathematical study of classical and quantum mechanics, her most widely cited work involves the area of mathematical physics known as wavelets, a mathematical way of dealing with symbols. Her work with wavelets has been used in the storage of FBI fingerprint files.

WOMEN IN TECHNOLOGY

1815–1852

Ada Byron Lovelace   England   Computer Scientist

Acknowledged as the world's first computer programmer, she wrote the first program that calculated Bernoulli numbers. She was also instrumental in the development of artificial intelligence. The first computer language was named after her, the ADA.

1883–1959

Edith Clarke   USA   Engineer

First woman to earn an MS degree at MIT. One of her greatest triumphs, as an employee of GE, was filing a patent for a "graphical calculator." Clark also broke ground when she became the first woman to teach engineering at the University of Texas in Austin during the 1940s.

1900–1986

Ida Rhodes   Ukraine   Computer Programmer

A pioneer in the development of the modern electronic digital computer and its use for numerical calculations.

1906–1992

Grace Murray Hopper   USA   Computer Compiler

Third programmer on the first computer in the United States, the Mark I. Known as one of the computer pioneers, she invented the first computer "compiler" in 1952. Credited with coining the term "bug" in reference to a glitch in the machinery, her contributions to computing paved the way for the production of UNIVAC I and II, the first commercial computers. During her years with the Navy, Hopper aided in the production of the COBOL computer language as well as translator programs to convert nonstandard COBOL languages into the standardized version.

1917–1990

Florence MacWilliams   England   Computer Programmer
Wrote one of the most powerful theorems in coding theory. Her equations are widely used by coding theorists. Best known for her book, The Theory of Error—Correcting Codes.

1918–1980

Alexandra Illmer Forsythe   USA   Computer Scientist
Coauthored a series of textbooks on computer science during the 1960s and 1970s.

Ca. 1920–

Thelma Estrin   USA   Engineer
One of the initial two engineers who designed and developed the WEIZAC in Israel, the world's first large-scale electronic computer outside of the United States and Western Europe.

1921–

Kay McNulty Mauchly Antonelli   USA   Computer Programmer
Employed along with about seventy-five other female mathematicians as a "computer" by the University of Pennsylvania's Moore School of Engineering. These "computers" were responsible for making calculations for tables of firing and bombing trajectories, as part of the war effort. The need to perform the calculations more quickly prompted the development of the ENIAC, the world's first electronic digital computer, in 1946.

1924–1980

Evelyn Boyd Granville   USA   Computer Programmer
One of the first African American women to earn a Ph.D. in Mathematics from Yale University. She developed computer programs that were used for trajectory analysis in the Mercury Project and in the Apollo Project.

1924–

Jean Bartik   USA   Computer Programmer
One of the team of young women who, in 1945, calculated trajectories to help wartime artillery gunners aim their weapons. She wrote the code that allowed the ENIAC to become a stored program computer.

?– 1964

Adele Goldstine   USA   Computer Scientist
Made a lasting contribution to the ENIAC project, the word's first electronic digital computer, by authoring the manual for the ENIAC in 1946. She also helped develop the object-oriented computing language, Smalltalk.

1927–2001

Betty Holberton   USA   Computer Programmer
One of the team of young women who, in 1945, calculated trajectories to help wartime artillery gunners aim their weapons. She also worked on the ENIAC, becoming one of the world's first programmers.

1928–

Jean E. Sammet   USA   Computer Programmer
Leading expert on the history of programming languages. She developed FORMAC, the first widely used language for manipulating symbolic mathematical expressions. She was also the first female president of the Association for Computing Machinery (ACM).

1932–

Fran Allen   USA   Computer Compiler
First woman to become a fellow at IBM's T. J. Watson Research Laboratory, and a pioneer in compiler optimization.

1933–

Annie Easley   USA   Computer Scientist
Developed and implemented computer code used in determining solar, wind, and energy projects for NASA. Her computer applications are used in the improvement of commercially available technology.

20th Century

Margaret R. Fox   USA   Electronics Engineer
Former chief of the Office of Computer Information in the NBS Institute for Computer Science and Technology 1966–1975.

20th Century

Erna Schneider Hoover   USA   Inventor
Invented a computerized switching system for telephone traffic and earned one of the first software patents ever issued. At Bell Labs, she became the first female supervisor of a technical department.

20th Century

Joan Margaret Winters   USA   Computer Programmer
Designed and implemented SPINDEX II applications for the Department of Manuscripts and University Archives at Cornell. In 1976, she joined SHARE's Human Factors Project, an IBM computer user group, and educated employees of IBM about the importance of software and conducting research into human factors and software tools.

20th Century

Judy Clapp   USA   Computer Programmer
Programmer of the world's first real-time control computer, the Whirlwind.

20th Century

Adele Mildred (Milly) Koss   USA   Computer Programmer
A programmer of the first commercial computer, the UNIVAC, she also designed and developed one of the first database systems to store and receive graphic images.

20th Century

Joyce Little   USA   Computer Scientist
A developer of one of the first curriculums for computer science, she was also one of the original programmers at Convair Aircraft Corporation in the Wind Tunnel Division.

20th Century

Ethel Marden   USA   Computer Programmer
Programmer of one of the first stored program computers, the SEAC.

GREAT WORDS OF

INSPIRATION

All of us need to inspire and be inspired by others. The following quotations from girls and women will serve as springboards for your own words and quotes. Which of these would most be like your thoughts? Write your own inspirational quotes and keep a record of them in a special journal or computer file. Revisit them often. Do your thoughts change over time?

GIRLS AND YOUNG WOMEN SPEAK OUT

These quotes were solicited anonymously from girls and young women. Which are your favorites?

*What advice would you give to girls today in pursuing
their goals in science, mathematics, or technology?*

"There are very few women in these fields today, and the job opportunities are absolutely endless. There are many positions to be filled by intelligent women. Don't let any stereotypes hold you back."

Ninth Grader

"I would tell them to go for it. If you try hard and tell yourself you can do it, you can succeed, and you will. It's a world full of surprises, but if you believe in yourself, you can do anything."

Seventh Grader

"I would advise them to first learn some history of these areas, and always try new things never ceasing to explore new areas. Do not let people with smaller minds keep you down, but most importantly, have confidence in your own mind. Never let someone lead you to believe you are average. There is no standard for normal. To make others believe in you, it is best to first believe in yourself."

Seventh Grader

"I would tell girls to not be afraid of math, science, and/or technology. Even though these things have been viewed as things guys do—girls can do them just as good, maybe even better. I encourage young girls to pursue their dreams with confidence."

Ninth Grader

"Follow your heart. If you want to become a rocket scientist or chemist, become a rocket scientist or chemist. It can sometimes be difficult for females to get into some of the scientific fields, and for those that do, they don't get enough credit."

Eighth Grader

"Never give up, believe in the power of a strong will. Remember, there's no such thing as an impossibility."

Seventh Grader

"A girl must be absolutely sure that she wants to succeed in pursuing her goals. There are many challenges up ahead and you'll face them all. None of it is as easy as you'll want it to be."

Seventh Grader

"Never let the lame stereotype 'Boys naturally do better than girls in math and science,' discourage your persistence and determination in pursuing your goals. Keep doing it and don't get discouraged."

Tenth Grader

"I would tell them to follow their dreams no matter what anyone else says. I mean after all, it's your choice and who are they to tell you what to do and what not to do? So just follow your dreams and do what you want."

Seventh Grader

"Girls often have ideas and structures that are more innovative and/or creative than boys and never get the chance to be acknowledged for their achievements, and we do deserve that. We must stand up to them all and prove that we are smart."

Seventh Grader

"If you want to pursue anything, whether it be science, math, technology, or anything, don't get discouraged with setbacks, and don't let anything stand in the way of your aspirations."

Seventh Grader

"If you're interested in math, science, or technology, then go for it. There's no reason why you can't do it."

Junior in College

"There is nothing to stop someone who pushes hard at what they are working for, especially in science or math. If there is promise in a person, no matter what their gender, then they can do whatever they wish. What the world actually could benefit from are more women in these careers."

Ninth Grader

"Many people stereotype the fields of math, science, and technology as being male-dominated facets in our culture. However, if anyone, male or female, strives to excel in these aspects, they can achieve the unfathomable."

Eighth Grader

"Prove all your critics wrong who say you can't do it because you're a girl, then they can only sing your praises."

Sophomore in College

"I would advise girls to overlook the ratio of boys to girls. We already know there will be one girl to several boys. I've experienced it myself. One has to realize that your interest in these subjects is based on knowledge and not gender."

Ninth Grader

"Even though women are often discriminated against in areas traditionally thought of as male careers, women have just as much right to pursue a career as a mathematician or a doctor as a man."

Ninth Grader

"Always try your hardest in all your subjects, study for all tests, never give up on yourself."

Seventh Grader

"Don't think you're at a disadvantage because you're a girl. Several girls now are dominating these areas in the outside world."

Eighth Grader

"You should work as hard as you can, don't be discouraged by those who don't encourage you, and take as many classes as you can in high school and aim high."

Eighth Grader

"Try your hardest and don't give up. When you get stuck ask a friend for help."

Seventh Grader

From whom have you found inspiration in pursuing math, science, and/or technology goals?

"My family doctor, who has been there since I was born, amazes me at the way he can cure a person with some horrible disease with only the help of schooling and a little lab equipment."

Ninth Grader

"My parents and teachers have gotten me interested in these areas. Both of my parents work in math/science fields, and they explain to me what they do. Good teachers always make math, science, and technology more interesting and make me want to learn more about them."

Eighth Grader

"I found inspiration for pursing math, science, and technology goals from my sixth grade teacher. She made science and technology fun, but she also showed us the serious side. She was a great inspiration because she encouraged me to decide to be whatever I wanted."

Seventh Grader

"My parents have always encouraged me to do well in math and science by making me do extra homework out of my textbook."

Seventh Grader

"I think my parents, especially my dad, and my teachers have helped me to want to reach my goals or even to have goals in those things. By telling me that I can do it if I want to and encouraging me to do it, but not making me do something that I don't want to."

Eighth Grader

"My mom always had a love for plants, in botany, horticulture, etc. She got me interested in biology because she had a passion for it, so when she talked about even the dullest of subjects, it was still interesting."

Seventh Grader

"My tenth grade chemistry teacher is the most organized, intelligent, and respected woman I know in the field of science. Every question that arose from lessons and class discussions were answered fully and explained."

Tenth Grader

"One person is my substitute teacher from elementary school that my mother and I have gotten close to. She was the first person to recognize my love for math, science, and astronomy and opened up my eyes to all these things at a young age, and I respect her for her ingenuity and generosity of her time with me."

Seventh Grader

"My dad, ever since I started school, has been behind me every step of the way. From the time I wanted to be an archaeologist to the thoughts of wanting to be a paleontologist. Everything I wanted to be, he was there every step of the way. He always told me that if there was something I wanted to be, strive to do it and be the best I could be."

Seventh Grader

"Actually, no one has stood in my way. It never occurred to me that I could not pursue math, science, or technology."

Junior in College

"My parents have really caused me to believe that work in science is the best possible field for me to enter. They have shown through science, not only are you helping others, but it can never get boring."

Ninth Grader

"It may sound bizarre but some of those who have inspired me most have been those who have little faith in my ability. I would strive for the element of surprise."

Eighth Grader

"I was the only girl in a room of about fifteen boys. The first part of the semester we learned the computer programming language BASIC. I soon found out that I was very good at it. The boys were coming to me for help."

Sophomore in College

"I guess I pretty much could say that everyone in my family inspires me. However, I could also say that it's just me, myself. I've always enjoyed doing well in school for me, it's a sense of pride and dignity, knowing that I'll go to an excellent college someday, and when I graduate, aside from my mom's and dad's proud faces, most of all I'll have satisfied myself and thought, 'I did it, I knew I could.'"

Seventh Grader

"My mother encourages me to do my best in my interest, math. My teacher was the first woman, other than my mother, that I saw who loved math."

Ninth Grader

"My seventh grade math teacher helped me in a way that I can't explain. I began to greatly enjoy math and got very good at it. Every year before that, I hated math and did horrible in it. It raised my self-esteem level and encouraged me to try my hardest in every subject."

Seventh Grader

"My cousin has encouraged me to consider civil engineering. My dad keeps me ahead in math because he hopes this will be my major and it is what I like to do best. My cousin was accepted from all of her job interviews, even over guys. This led me to hope one day I will have as good a chance as anyone."

Eighth Grader

"My teachers and parents have really encouraged me to try my hardest and do as much as possible. My friends also encourage me to work hard in school."

Eighth Grader

"Marie Curie is a good role model and great influence."

Seventh Grader

"My father, he has a great job that involves much of math, science, and technology. He always tries his hardest, and when he's stuck, he's not afraid to ask for help."

Seventh Grader

What are some of the special challenges that you feel girls and young women face today in pursuing careers in math, science, and technology-related fields? What words of inspiration would you give to such individuals as they encounter these challenges?

"Many girls find that being smart isn't 'cool.' When you grow up, that doesn't matter. No one will hire you because you were the 'coolest' person in your school."

Seventh Grader

"Many young women get less pay for equal work, are discriminated against in job interviews, and told that careers in math, science, and technology are not open to them. I would tell these girls to just keep working as hard as they can and not to give up."

Eighth Grader

"Personally, I no longer believe that girls are overlooked in society. They are given the same opportunities as men but a lot of them don't make it because they have bad attitudes. I believe that if you believe in yourself and don't give up, you will always reach your goal."

Seventh Grader

"Discrimination and ridicule are big challenges. Equal pay is also a challenge."

Ninth Grader

"As before, standardized tests are more geared toward boys. You just have to be more prepared and work harder to reach your goal."

Ninth Grader

"Girls face challenges pursuing careers in these areas everyday. They face the workplace, knowing they're the only woman or one in a small percentage. They face the intimidation of the presence of men, and the negative comments of 'This is a man's profession.'"

Ninth Grader

"I think that in math, science, and technology fields, girls undergo a lot of underestimation, and there's still a lot of sexism and racism in the world. Maybe we can't change all of it, but we can make the world realize that we are every bit as good in these careers as men."

Seventh Grader

"Prejudices arise against many girls who display an interest in a 'man's job.' Some foster the predilection towards males and assume that females aren't competent enough to excel. For me, this just adds fuel to my fire and strengthens my desire to learn."

Eighth Grader

"The greatest challenge of all is to prove yourself more as an individual with new ideas and promise than as a woman. One must get past the discrimination people have placed upon another."

Ninth Grader

"Some still feel that women have no place in math, science, or technology. I say, don't listen. If you take that in and believe it, then you will never be able to do it. Have faith in yourself and your abilities. Don't sell yourself short; you can do anything you put your mind to."

Junior in College

"Everybody has certain challenges they face in anything. I don't think there are any challenges that anybody has except their own self-confidence."

Seventh Grader

"In these fields it has been limited to just men until recently. Women are still trying to break through the barriers. When encountering these challenges, remember you're just as good as any guy out there, maybe even better. As long as you work on what you want, you can accomplish anything."

Seventh Grader

"In this day and age, our society is still being dominated by men. In most parts of the country, women are still earning about 70 percent of what men get for the same work. Although, I think that it's widely accepted that women are the fairer sex, and we will work hard and continue to stand out until our rights are equal."

Seventh Grader

"The only words I can say are to stand up to those challenges and push yourself even harder so that you can attain your goal."

Ninth Grader

"I think we are given the same challenges as all. Discrimination, doubt, disrespect. We must always believe we can make a difference, if only to one person."

Seventh Grader

What do your parents and friends think about your interest in math, science, or technology?

"My dad and mom really encourage me because math, science, and technology are the career fields of the future. They want me to succeed in life."

Ninth Grader

"My parents and friends think that it is great that I am interested in becoming a marine biologist. They tell me to go for my dreams and that I will succeed."

Seventh Grader

"My parents are very supportive. They want me to do what I love and encourage me to think in new ways and defy the usual crowd."

Seventh Grader

"My parents really encourage my interest in math, science, and technology. They know that a lot of jobs need these three things, and they strongly encourage me to pursue my goals."

Ninth Grader

"My family and friends are all very supportive of my interests and feminist beliefs. [On attending an academic summer program] I have been receiving a daily stream of letters, notes, and cards from church members and all of those I love. Every single one went on about how proud they were of me and what a great opportunity it was. My grandmother is very old-fashioned and believes that young ladies should be very proper, and she was raised during times when women were treated nothing like men. I have no problems with that, but just the same, I'm glad that times are changing and someday we'll know a truly equal society and no one will know oppression."

Seventh Grader

"Everyone thinks it's a great idea! Women are no longer restricted to pursuing careers. I am taking advantage of this fact and no one is stopping me from advancing my knowledge in math/science/technology fields. It is going to be a new trend!"

Tenth Grader

"My mother knows that I either want to be a mathematical engineer or astronomical engineer when I grow up and so do my friends, but my mother recognizes my interest and helps me through it all. She tries to inspire and encourage me and is always there, and I am truly grateful for that."

Seventh Grader

"My parents and friends are my main source of support. They have encouraged and inspired me to do my best at anything I do, whether it be science, math, English, social studies, or anything for that matter. They have all wished the best for me."

Seventh Grader

"My friends and parents like and support me no matter what my interest. My parents never doubted my possible abilities in math, science, or technology. Rather, my parents always pushed me to do my best and to learn all I could. These fields were not treated as improper for me or as extra difficult. Because of their attitude, I never viewed these fields that way—I never had any barriers to math, science, or technology."

Junior in College

"Everyone I have spoken to about this subject has respected and encouraged my thoughts and goals of working in the scientific field."

Ninth Grader

"My friends think of me as a little crazy when I skip school parties and things to devote time to my studies. My parents are pretty much thrilled when I show interest in math and science, especially since they've both worked in these before. It makes them feel proud that their daughter is following in their footsteps."

Seventh Grader

"My mom loves it. We share a common interest. My friends sometimes don't understand it. They don't understand why I pursue it, but they still encourage me."

Ninth Grader

"My parents are very happy that I am excited about math and are doing everything they can to help me when I need it."

Seventh Grader

"My parents encourage me to do anything that will make me happy. They encourage me to excel in school and be ambitious. My friends also want to have careers in technology, so they encourage me, too."

Eighth Grader

"They are very proud of the devotion I have, of the skills I have, and how hard I work on developing them."

Seventh Grader

PROFESSIONAL WOMEN SPEAK OUT

Adult females, past and present, have great words of inspiration. Which are your favorites?

"If you are interested in a subject and have a desire to pursue it, you can achieve anything. Don't be discouraged by the opinions of others or their biases. If there are no female role models, take a male as a role model. Someday you may be a role model to a boy who admires your achievements."

Sharon Alden
Lead Forecaster/Meteorologist
National Weather Service/Pocatello, Idaho

"Pursuing a career in math, science, and technology should no longer be a male-dominated endeavor; with new interdisciplinary fields evolving and high-tech becoming a part of daily life, now more than ever, it is important for women to take up careers in these fields."

Sheela V. Belur
Computer Scientist
Computer Sciences Corporation (CSC)

"Methods and conclusions formed by half the race only, must necessarily require revision as the other half of humanity rises into conscious responsibility."

Elizabeth Blackwell
First Female American Doctor

"If a child is to keep alive his inborn sense of wonder, he needs the companionship of at least one adult who can share it, rediscovering with him the joy, excitement and mystery of the world we live in."

Rachel Carson
Zoologist, Author, and Environmentalist

"I am angry at the condition of a society that creates problems for blacks and for women. But I think there are ways anger can be turned into something positive."

Jewel Plummer Cobb
Cell Biologist

"Creativity is inventing, experimenting, growing, taking risks, breaking rules, making mistakes and having fun."

Mary Lou Cook
Environmentalist

"Life is not easy for any of us. But what of that? We must have perseverance and above all confidence in ourselves. We must believe that we are gifted for something, and that this thing, at whatever cost, must be attained."

Marie Curie
Physicist

"Always make new mistakes!"

Esther Dyson
Chairman, Edventure Holdings
Chairman, Internet Corp. for Assigned Names and Numbers

"It never occurred to me any more than to a man that I'd stop and turn off my mind because I had children. I think that because I had a strong feeling about what I wanted to do, it enabled me to continue. I never thought of it as unusual."

Sylvia Earle
Marine Biologist, Environmentalist, and Diver

"Don't be afraid to be challenged. Don't be afraid to be wrong, just be prepared to admit it. Don't be afraid to stand up for yourself and be assertive. Do a job shadow of someone in the career you think you might want to do. Find out what that person does on a daily basis. . . . Be prepared and you will be able to do what you want when you decide what that is."

Lori Freeman
Analytical Lab Manager/Clinical Lab
Micron Technology, Inc.

"Often in careers there are choices to be made—where to go to college, where to go to graduate school, what job to take—and those choices can seem very difficult to make. I, however, think that successful people do not succeed because of their choices, but rather because they make the most of the opportunities available to them no matter where they end up."

Andrea Ghez
Professor of Physics and Astronomy

"Artists use the science behind their art to pursue their passion for the particular, a means of cresting something unique that moves us. Scientists use their art of observation and analysis to pursue a passion for the principle, that insight that shines light on what was previously not understood. To find your passion, you need skills in both science and the humanities. Study both and you will find the focus right for you."

Katherine Hammer
President and CEO
Evolutionary Technologies International

"If you do something once, people will call it an accident. If you do it twice, they call it coincidence. But do it a third time and you've just proven natural law."

Grace Murray Hopper
Mathematician and Pioneer in Data Processing

"Research is formalized curiosity. It is poking and prying with a purpose."

Zora Neale Hurston
Anthropologist

"I very much believe success is a personal thing, very much dependent on how much a person deals with and approaches both opportunities and crises."

Millie J. Kronflu
Aerospace Engineer

"Nothing can really compare to the value of having role models. Even just one really good role model is worth her weight in gold. Someone that you can relate to, someone who is in exactly the same place you are or has been there before. Someone that you can hold yourself up against and say, if she can do it, I can do it too. "

Jennifer Lai
Pervasive Computing
IBM Research

[On receiving the Nobel Prize] "It might seem unfair to reward a person for having so much pleasure over the years, asking the maize plant to solve specific problems and then watching its responses. I can't imagine a better life."

Barbara McClintock
American Geneticist

"Winning the prize [1963 Nobel Prize in physics] wasn't half as exciting as doing the work itself."

Maria Goeppert Mayer
Physicist

"If we are to achieve richer culture, rich in contrasting values, we must recognize the whole gamut of human potentialities, and so weave a less arbitrary social fabric, one in which each diverse human gift will find a fitting place."

Margaret Mead
Anthropologist

"In my younger days, when I was pained by the half-educated, loose and inaccurate ways women had, I used to say, 'How much women need exact science.' But since I have known some workers in science, I have now said, 'How much science needs women.'"

Maria Mitchell
First American Female Astronaut

"We will have equality when a female schlemiel moves ahead as fast as a male schlemiel."

Dr. Estelle Ramey
First Female Medical Professor at Georgetown University

"The environment that people live in is the environment that they learn to live in, respond to, and perpetuate. If the environment is good, so be it. But if it is poor, so is the quality of life within it."

Ellen Swallow Richards
American Chemist

"You can achieve great things by . . . being willing to learn new things, being able to assimilate new information quickly, and being able to get along with and work with other people."

Sally Ride
American Astronaut

"If you enjoy challenge and want to make a contribution to society, science and technology provide great opportunity. When your parents were your age, there were no women astronauts and there were few women scientists. There are still glass ceilings and sticky floors for scientists, so you can expect to do some pioneering, but our country has always valued pioneers."

Sylvia Rimm
American Psychologist and Author

"If I didn't believe the answer could be found, I wouldn't be working on it."

Florence Sabin
American Anatomist

"Learn as much as you can—in school, through work experience, from mentors who have accomplished things you are interested in. Listen to their stories and understand that for most people, achieving your dreams is within your reach if you are willing to work hard to get there. Life is a series of challenges, and the quality of your life—the success of your life—is determined by how you face those challenges. When things don't work out the way you had hoped, think of it as a learning experience rather than a failure and take from it what you can to make your next venture more likely to work. Never let someone tell you 'no.' No matter how hard it gets, or how dark it gets, keep going, because if you don't give up, you'll win. That's the secret to success."

Janese Swanson
Founder, Senior Vice President
Girl Tech

"We still live in a world in which a significant fraction of people, including women, believe that a woman belongs and wants to belong exclusively in the home."

Rosalyn Sussman Yalow
Medical Physicist

"Every strong, successful woman I know draws from some deep inner strength during difficult times. What makes them special to me is this special quality of resilience while still maintaining feminine compassion."

Petra R. Scheider-Redden
Plastic Surgeon

"Since you only pass through this world once, accept life's challenge to do your very best. Each day is an opportunity; learn from each and every experience."

Virginia Angelico Tatum
Dentist

JOURNAL

Journaling provides a valuable means for documenting your accomplishments, setting future goals, and cataloging new knowledge and materials relating to science, mathematics, and technology. The following pages provide some sample journal entries that you might consider. Can you think of other activities to add?

LOG
SCIENCE/MATH/TECHNOLOGY

Name: _____

Date: _____

Topic: _____

❑ Science ❑ Math ❑ Technology

Goal Statement: _____

_____

_____

What I would like to accomplish: _____

_____

_____

_____

_____

What I have accomplished to date:_____

_____

_____

_____

_____

What I will need to do next:_____

_____

_____

_____

Estimated completion date:_____

_____

_____

Signature

STUDENT INVENTORY
SCIENCE/MATH/TECHNOLOGY

You will accomplish many important goals in science/math/technology over the coming years. Recording your accomplishments will help you have a permanent record.

Student _____

Date	Accomplishment	Subject Area	Grade Level

HOW I FEEL ABOUT MY WORK IN SCIENCE/MATH/TECHNOLOGY

Your feelings have a lot to do with your work in science/math/technology. Recording your emotions will give you insights about yourself.

In science, I feel _____

_____

_____

_____

_____

_____

_____

_____

In math, I feel _____

_____

_____

_____

_____

_____

_____

In technology, I feel _____

_____

_____

_____

_____

_____

_____

_____

HALL OF FAME
SCIENCE/MATH/TECHNOLOGY

Nomination Form

There are hundreds of outstanding females in science/math/technology. Nominate one in each area for the hall of fame.

Nominee	Area of Science/Math/Technology	Reason(s) for Nomination

My Favorite Books
Science/Math/Technology

There are many great books on these topics. Think about *your* favorite ones and why you like them.

My favorite books and why I liked them!

Author:_____ Title:_____

Why I like this book: _____

_____

_____

Author:_____ Title:_____

Why I like this book: _____

_____

_____

Author:_____ Title:_____

Why I like this book: _____

_____

_____

Author:_____ Title:_____

Why I like this book: _____

_____

_____

Author:_____ Title:_____

Why I like this book: _____

_____

_____

MY ROLE MODEL IN
SCIENCE/MATH/TECHNOLOGY

There are many girls and women who are outstanding in these areas. After reading several biographies that interest you, select one as your role model and describe the reasons why.

My role model is _____

_____

She is my role model because _____

_____

_____

_____

_____

_____

_____

_____

_____

_____

_____

_____

_____

_____

_____

_____

_____

_____

_____

_____

_____

_____

_____

_____

_____

_____

WHY I WANT TO BE OUTSTANDING IN SCIENCE/MATH/TECHNOLOGY

There may be many great reasons for wanting to be outstanding in science, math, or technology. Think about the inspiring stories you have read in this book. What are some of the reasons for entering these fields given by the girls? Write as many as you can now; add more later. What are some of your own personal reasons?

★ _____

_____

_____

★ _____

_____

_____

★ _____

_____

_____

★ _____

_____

_____

★ _____

_____

_____

★ _____

_____

_____

★ _____

_____

_____

★ _____

_____

_____

★ _____

_____

_____

★ _____

_____

_____

★ _____

_____

_____

MY CALENDAR FOR ACHIEVING IN SCIENCE/MATH/TECHNOLOGY

Developing a schedule for success in science/math/technology is important in achieving goals. Use this schedule or put one on a calendar or in your computer.

Days of Week	Great Things to Do
Sunday	
Monday	
Tuesday	
Wednesday	
Thursday	
Friday	
Saturday	

PLACES WHERE I HAVE SHARED MY GREAT WORK IN SCIENCE/MATH/TECHNOLOGY

There are many places where you can share your accomplishments in science/math/technology. You can display projects in your school or community. Magazines and professional journals are great places to submit written descriptions and photographs. Keeping a record will help you remember your many accomplishments.

Project	Place	Date	Comments

WHAT I HAVE LEARNED ABOUT MYSELF WHILE WORKING IN SCIENCE/MATH/TECHNOLOGY

Setting your goals to be outstanding in science/math/technology helps you envision many exciting things about yourself.

Interests:

_____

_____

Strengths:

_____

_____

Areas Needing Strengthening:

_____

_____

Abilities:

_____

_____

Work Habits:

_____

_____

Resourcefulness:

_____

_____

Attitudes:

_____

_____

Planning Skills:

_____

_____

Research Skills:

_____

_____

Computer Skills:

_____

_____

Writing Skills:

_____

_____

Time Management Skills:

_____

_____

GREAT QUOTATIONS
SCIENCE/MATH/TECHNOLOGY

The quotations in this book on science/math/technology given by out-standing females offer words of knowledge and inspiration. Select the one that means the most to you and tell why. Record your quote and share it with others.

My favorite quote is_____

_____

_____

_____

_____

The reason this quote means the most to me is _____

_____

_____

_____

_____

My inspiring quotation on science/math/technology is _____

_____

_____

_____

_____

I will share it with the following persons:

_____

_____

_____

_____

COMPETITIONS
SCIENCE/MATH/TECHNOLOGY

There are many competitions in science/math/technology at all grade levels and for both genders. Most begin at the local or regional levels and then proceed to state and national events. Keep a record of your options on the form below or start a file in your computer.

Competition: _____

Mailing Address:_____

City, State, Zip Code:_____

Web site: _____

E-mail: _____

Date of Application: _____

Application Fee, if any: _____

Date of Event:_____

Location of Event: _____

Award/Prize/Recognition: _____

For more information on competitions consult: Karnes, F.A., & Riley, T.L. (1996). *Competitions: Maximizing Your Abilities.* Waco, TX: Prufrock Press.

Part IV

BOOKS FOR GIRLS &
YOUNG WOMEN

In Science,
Mathematics,
and Technology

Books offer information and details on the lives of girls and women in science, mathematics, and technology. The following reference listings are divided into two sections: One for elementary school girls and another for young women in secondary school and beyond. Some of the books are specific to women in science, mathematics, and technology; others offer insight into general aspects of these three areas including information on careers. Look for additional volumes on the Internet and in the libraries and bookstores in your town or community. Share your favorite books with your sisters, female cousins, and friends. Perhaps your parents will enjoy knowing the ones you like best. Consider reading passages from your favorites to younger girls to help inspire and motivate them toward their goals in science, mathematics, and technology.

BOOKS FOR GIRLS

Accorsi, William. *Rachel Carson*. New York: Holiday House, 1993.

Adler, David A. *A Picture Book of Florence Nightingale*. New York: Holiday House, 1997.

Andryszewski, Tricia. *Marjory Stoneman Douglas: Friend of the Everglades*. Brookfield, Conn.: Millbrook, 1994.

Anholt, Laurence. *Stone Girl, Bone Girl: The Story of Mary Anning*. New York: Orchard, 1999.

Ashby, Ruth. *Herstory: Women Who Changed the World*. New York: Viking, 1995.

Atkins, Jeannine. *Mary Anning and the Sea Dragon*. New York: Farrar, Straus, & Giroux, 1999.

Baker, Rachel. *The First Woman Doctor: The Story of Elizabeth Blackwell, M.D.* New York: Scholastic, 1995.

Barry, David. *The Rajah's Rice: A Mathematical Folktale from India*. New York: W. H. Freeman & Company, 1994.

Behrens, June. *Sally Ride, Astronaut: An American First*. Danbury, Conn.: Children's Press, 1984.

Billings, Charlene W. *Grace Hopper: Navy Admiral and Computer Pioneer*. Hillside, N.J.: Enslow, 1989.

Bozak, Kristin, and Judith Love Cohen. *You Can Be a Woman Botanist*. Culver City, Calif.: Cascade Pass, 1999.

Bredeson, Carmen. *Shannon Lucid: Space Ambassador*. Brookfield, Conn.: Millbrook, 1998.

Briggs, Carole S. *At the Controls: Women in Aviation*. Minneapolis, Minn.: Lerner, 1991.

Briggs, Carole S. *Women in Space*. Minneapolis, Minn.: Lerner, 1998.

Brown, Don. *Rare Treasure: Mary Anning and Her Remarkable Discoveries*. Boston: Houghton Mifflin, 1999.

Brown, Jordan. *Elizabeth Blackwell*. Broomall, Pa.: Chelsea House, 1989.

Bryant, Jennifer Fisher. *Marjory Stoneman Douglas: Voice of the Everglades*. Brookfield, Conn.: Twenty-First Century Books, 1992.

Bursztynski, Sue. *Potions to Pulsars: Women Doing Science*. Chicago: Independent Publishers Group, 1996.

Campbell, Robin. *Florence Sabin: Scientist*. Broomall, Pa.: Chelsea House, 1995.

Casey, Susan. *Women Invent: Two Centuries of Discoveries That Have Shaped Our World*. Chicago: Chicago Review Press, 1997.

Cohen, Judith Love. *You Can Be a Woman Engineer*. Culver City, Calif.: Cascade Pass, 1996.

Cohen, Judith Love, and Andrea M. Ghez. *You Can Be a Woman Astronomer.* Culver City, Calif.: Cascade Pass, 1998.

Cohen, Judith Love, and Margot Seigel. *You Can Be a Woman Architect.* Culver City, Calif.: Cascade Pass, 1999.

Colver, Anne. *Florence Nightingale: War Nurse.* Broomall, Pa.: Chelsea House, 1992.

Conley, Andrea. *Window on the Deep: The Adventures of Underwater Explorer Sylvia Earle.* Danbury, Conn.: Franklin Watts, 1991.

Dewey, Jennifer Owens. *Wildlife Rescue: The Work of Dr. Kathleen Ramsay.* Honesdale, Pa.: Boyds Mills, 1994.

Dickinson, Peter. *A Bone from a Dry Sea.* New York: Dell, 1995.

Ferris, Jeri. *Native American Doctor: The Story of Susan Laflesche Picotte.* Minneapolis, Minn.: Lerner, 1991.

Fisher, Leonard Everett. *Marie Curie.* New York: Macmillan, 1994.

Franks, Sharon, and Judith Love Cohen. *You Can Be a Woman Oceanographer.* Culver City, Calif.: Cascade Pass, 1994.

Fromer, Julie. *Jane Goodall: Living With the Chimps.* Brookfield, Conn.: Twenty-First Century Books, 1992.

Gabriel, Diane L., and Judith Love Cohen. *You Can Be a Woman Paleontologist.* Culver City, Calif.: Cascade Pass, 1999.

Gallardo, Evelyn. *Among the Orangutans: The Birute Galdikas Story.* San Francisco: Chronicle Books, 1993.

Goldberg, Jane. *Rachel Carson.* Broomall, Pa.: Chelsea House, 1991.

Goodall, J. *My Life with the Chimpanzees.* New York: Pocket Books, 1996.

Greene, Carol. *Elizabeth Blackwell: First Woman Doctor.* Danbury, Conn.: Children's Press, 1991.

———. *Marie Curie: Pioneer Physicist.* Danbury, Conn.: Children's Press, 1984.

Hacker, Carlotta. *Nobel Prize Winners: Women in Profile Series.* New York: Crabtree, 1998.

———. *Scientists: Women in Profile Series.* New York: Crabtree, 1998.

Heiligman, Deborah. *Barbara McClintock: Alone in Her Field.* New York: W. H. Freeman & Company, 1994.

Henry, Joanne. *Elizabeth Blackwell: Girl Doctor.* Madison, Wis.: Demco Media, 1996.

Horenstein, Henry. *My Mom's a Vet.* Cambridge, Mass.: Candlewick, 1994.

Ingoglia, Gina. *Amanda Visits the Planets.* New York: G. T. Publishing, 1998.

Johnson, Rebecca L. *Braving the Frozen Frontier: Women Working in Antarctica.* Minneapolis, Minn.: Lerner, 1996.

Kennedy, Don H. *Little Sparrow: A Portrait of Sophia Kovalevsky.* Athens, Ohio: Ohio University Press, 1983.

Kronstadt, Janet. *Florence Sabin: Medical Researcher.* Broomall, Pa.: Chelsea House, 1990.

Krull, Kathleen. *Lives of Extraordinary Women: Rulers, Rebels (and What the Neighbors Thought).* New York: Harcourt, 2000.

Kudlinski, Kathleen. *Rachel Carson: Pioneer of Ecology.* New York: Penguin Putnam Books for Young Readers, 1997.

Latham, Jean Lee. *Elizabeth Blackwell: Pioneer Woman Doctor.* Broomall, Pa.: Chelsea House, 1991.

——. *Rachel Carson: Who Loved the Sea.* Broomall, Pa.: Chelsea House, 1997.

Lauber, Patricia. *Lost Star: The Story of Amelia Earhart.* New York: Scholastic, 1988.

Lepscky, Ibi. *Marie Curie.* Hauppauge, N.Y.: Barron's Educational Series, 1993.

Lindop, Laurie. *Scientists and Doctors: Dynamic Modern Women.* Brookfield, Conn.: Twenty-First Century Books, 1997.

Marsh, Carole. *Math for Girls: The Book with the Number on Getting Girls to Love and Excel in Math!* Peachtree City, Ga.: Gallopade International, 1994.

McAlary, Florence, and Judith Love Cohen. *You Can Be a Woman Marine Biologist.* Culver City, Calif.: Cascade Pass, 1997.

McGovern, Ann. *Shark Lady: True Adventures of Eugenie Clark.* New York: Four Winds, 1978.

McPherson, Stephanie S. *Rooftop Astronomer: A Story about Maria Mitchell.* Minneapolis, Minn.: Carolrhoda Books, 1990.

——. *The Workers' Detective: A Story about Dr. Alice Hamilton.* Minneapolis, Minn.: Carolrhoda Books, 1992.

Morrissey, Muriel. *Amelia Earhart.* San Francisco: Bellerophon, 1977.

Murrows, Liza Ketchum. *Susan Humphris: Geologist.* Brattleboro, Vt.: Teachers Laboratory, 1989.

Parker, Steve. *Marie Curie and Radium.* Broomall, Pa.: Chelsea House, 1995.

Parlin, John. *Amelia Earhart.* Broomall, Pa.: Chelsea House, 1992.

Patterson, Francine. *Koko's Story.* New York: Scholastic, 1987.

Pflaum, Rosalynd. *Marie Curie and Her Daughter Irene.* Minneapolis, Minn.: Lerner, 1993.

Powell, Mary Curtner. *Queen of the Air: The Story of Katherine Stinson 1891–1977.* Dallas: Coldwater, 1993.

Pringle, Laurence. *Jackal Woman: Exploring the World of Jackals.* New York: Scribner, 1993.

——. *Elephant Woman: Cynthia Moss Explores the World of Elephants.* New York: Atheneum Books for Young Readers, 1997.

Quackenbush, Robert. *Clear the Cow Pasture, I'm Coming in for a Landing!: A Story of Amelia Earhart.* New York: Simon & Schuster, 1990.

———. *Clara Barton and Her Victory Over Fear.* New York: Simon & Schuster, 1995.

Ransom, Candice. *Listening to Crickets: A Story about Rachel Carson.* Minneapolis, Minn: Lerner, 1993.

Redberg, Rita, and Judith Love Cohen. *You Can Be a Woman Cardiologist.* Culver City, Calif.: Cascade Pass, 1996.

Ride, Sally, and Susan Oakie. *To Space and Back.* New York: Lothrop, Lee, & Shepard, 1986.

Ring, Elizabeth. *Rachel Carson: Caring for the Earth.* Brookfield, Conn.: Millbrook 1994.

Romanek, Trudee. *The Technology Book for Girls and Other Advanced Beings.* Buffalo, N.Y.: Kids Can Press.

Rose, Mary Catherine. *Clara Barton: Soldier of Mercy.* Broomall, Pa.: Chelsea House, 1991.

Saari, Peggy. *Prominent Women of the Twentieth Century.* Farmington Hills, Mich.: Gale Group, 1995.

———. *Women's Chronology: A History of Women's Achievements.* Farmington Hills, Mich.: Gale Group, 1997.

———. *Women's Firsts: Milestones in Women's History.* Farmington Hills, Mich.: Gale Group, 1997.

Sakurai, Gail. *Mae Jemison: Space Scientist.* Danbury, Conn.: Children's Press, 1995.

Schloss, Muriel. *Mary Cleave: Astronaut.* Brattleboro. Vt.: Teachers' Laboratory, 1990.

Scott, Elaine. *Adventure in Space: The Flight to Fix the Hubble.* New York: Hyperion Paperbacks for Children, 1995.

Siegel, Beatrice. *Faithful Friend: The Story of Florence Nightingale.* New York: Scholastic, 1991.

Steinke, Ann E. *Marie Curie and the Discovery of Radium.* Hauppage, N.Y.: Barron's Educational Series, 1987.

Stevenson, Augusta. *Clara Barton: Founder of the American Red Cross.* Madison, Wis.: Demco Media, 1986.

Thimmish, Catherine. *Girls Think of Everything.* New York: Houghton Mifflin, 2000.

Tucker, Tom. *Brainstorm: The Stories of Twenty American Kid Inventors.* New York: Farrar, Straus, & Giroux, 1998.

Van Meter, Vicki. *Taking Flight: My Story.* New York: Viking, 1995.

Vare, Ethlie Ann. *Adventurous Spirit: A Story about Ellen Swallow Richards.* Minneapolis, Minn.: Carolrhoda Books, 1992.

Vare, Ethlie Ann, and Greg Ptacek. *Women Inventors and Their Discoveries.* Minneapolis, Minn: Oliver, 1993.

Verheyden-Hilliard, Mary Ellen. *Engineer from the Comanche Nation: Nancy Wallace.* Bethesda, Md.: Equity Institute, 1985.

————. *Mathematician and Administrator: Shirley Mathis McBay.* Bethesda, Md.: Equity Institute, 1985.

————. *Scientist and Administrator: Antionette Rodez Schiesler.* Bethesda, Md.: Equity Institute, 1985.

————. *Scientist and Astronaut: Sally Ride.* Bethesda, Md.: Equity Institute, 1985.

————. *Scientist and Governor: Dixy Lee Ray.* Bethesda, Md.: Equity Institute, 1985.

————. *Scientist and Planner: Ru Chih Cheo Huang.* Bethesda, Md.: Equity Institute, 1985.

————. *Scientist and Puzzle Solver: Constance Toni Noguchi.* Bethesda, Md.: Equity Institute, 1985.

————. *Scientist from Puerto Rico: Maria Cordero Hardy.* Bethesda, Md.: Equity Institute, 1985.

————. *Scientist from the Santa Clara Pueblo: Agnes Naranjo Stroud-Lee.* Bethesda, Md.: Equity Institute, 1985.

————. *Scientist with Determination: Elma Gonzales.* Bethesda, Md.: Equity Institute, 1985.

————. *American Women in Science Biographies.* Vols. 1–15. Bethesda, Md.: Equity Institute, 1988.

————. *Mathematician and Computer Scientist: Caryn Navy.* Bethesda, Md.: Equity Institute, 1988.

————. *Scientist and Activist: Phyllis Stearner.* Bethesda, Md.: Equity Institute, 1988.

————. *Scientist and Physician: Judith Pachciarz.* Bethesda, Md.: Equity Institute, 1988.

————. *Scientist and Strategist: June Rooks.* Bethesda, Md.: Equity Institute, 1988.

————. *Scientist and Teacher: Anne Barrett Swanson.* Bethesda, Md.: Equity Institute, 1988.

Wadsworth, Ginger. *Rachel Carson: Voice for the Earth.* Minneapolis, Minn.: Lerner, 1992.

Wells, Rosemary. *Mary on Horseback: Three Mountain Stories.* New York: Penguin Putnam Books for Young Readers, 1998.

Whitelaw, Nancy. *Grace Hopper: Programming Pioneer.* New York: W. H. Freeman & Company, 1995.

Winegarten, Ruthe, and Sharon Kahn. *Brave Black Women: From Slavery to the Space Shuttle.* Austin, Tex.: University of Texas Press, 1997.

Wyatt, Valerie. *The Science Book for Girls and Other Intelligent Beings.* Buffalo, N.Y.: Kids Can Press, 1997.

BOOKS FOR YOUNG WOMEN

Alic, Margaret. *Hypatia's Heritage: A History of Women in Science from Antiquity to the Nineteenth Century.* London: Women's Press, 1986.

Alcot, Sarah. *Young Clara Barton: Battlefield Nurse.* Mahwah, N.J.: Troll, 1997.

Altman, Linda Jacobs. *Women Inventors.* New York: Facts on File, 1997.

American Association of University Women. *Shortchanging Girls, Shortchanging America: A Call to Action.* Washington, D.C.: Author, 1991.

Arnold, Lois B. *Four Lives in Science: Women's Education in the Nineteenth Century.* New York: Schocken, 1984.

Baldwin, Joyce. *To Heal the Heart of a Child: Helen Taussig, M.D.* New York: Walker, 1992.

Baldwin, Richard. *The Fungus Fighters: Two Women Scientists and Their Discovery.* Ithaca, N.Y.: Cornell University Press, 1981.

Bindocci, Cynthia Gay. *Women and Technology: An Annotated Bibliography.* Vol. 517, Garland Reference Library of Social Science. Levittown, Pa.: Garland, 1993.

Bonta, Marcia M. *Women in the Field: America's Pioneering Women Naturalists.* College Station, Tex.: Texas A & M Press, 1992.

———. *American Women Afield: Writings by Pioneering Women Naturalists.* College Station, Tex.: Texas A & M Press, 1995.

Breton, Mary Joy. *Women Pioneers for the Environment.* Boston: Northeastern University Press, 1998.

Brill, Marlene Targ. *Extraordinary Young People.* Danbury, Conn.: Children's Press, 1996.

Byrne, Eileen. *Women and Science: The Snark Syndrome.* Levittown, Pa.: Falmer, 1993.

Cole, Sheila. *The Dragon in the Cliff: A Novel Based on the Life of Mary Anning.* New York: Lothrop, Lee & Shepard, 1991.

Curie, Eve. *Madame Curie: A Biography.* Translated by V. Sheean. New York: Da Capo, 1986.

Dossey, Barbara Montgomery. *Florence Nightingale: Mystic, Visionary, Healer.* Springhouse, Pa.: Springhouse, 1999.

Douglass, Emily Taft. *Margaret Sanger: Pioneer of the Future.* Chicago: Ferguson, 1991.

Etzkowitz, Henry, Carol Kemelgor, and Brian Uzzi. *Athena Unbound: The Advancement of Women in Science and Technology.* Oxford: Cambridge University Press, 2000.

Faruqui, A. M, ed. *Role of Women in the Development of Science and Technology in the Third World: Proceedings of the Conference Organized by the Canadian International.* River Edge, N.J.: World Scientific, 1991.

Foundation Center. *National Guide to Funding for Women and Girls.* New York: Foundation Center, 1999.

Furger, Roberta. *Does Jane Compute?: Preserving Our Daughters' Place in the Cyber Revolution.* New York: Warner, 1998.

Gattiker, Urs, ed. *Women and Technology. Vol. 4, Technological Innovation and Human Resources.* Hawthorne, N.Y.: Walter De Gruyter, 1994.

Glimm, Adele. *Elizabeth Blackwell: First Woman Doctor of Modern Times.* New York: McGraw-Hill, 2000.

Goodall, Jane. *In the Shadow of Man.* Boston: Houghton Mifflin, 1988.

———. *Through a Window: My Thirty Years with the Chimpanzees of Gombe.* Boston: Houghton Mifflin, 1990.

Gornik, Vivian. *Women in Science: Portraits from a World in Transition.* New York: Simon & Schuster, 1990.

Green, Richard L. *Black Scientists and Inventors: A Gift of Heritage.* Chicago: Empak Enterprises, 1992.

Green, Robert, and Hedda Garza. *Women of Medicine.* New York: Franklin Watts, 1994.

Grinstein, Louise S., and Carol A. Biermann, eds. *Women in the Biological Sciences: A Bibliographic Sourcebook.* Westport, Conn.: Greenwood, 1997.

Grinstein, Louise S., and Paul Campbell, eds. *Women of Mathematics: A Bibliographic Sourcebook.* Westport, Conn.: Greenwood, 1987.

Grossman, Herbert. *Gender Issues in Education.* Boston: Allyn and Bacon, 1993.

Hamerstrom, Frances. *My Double Life: Memoirs of a Naturalist.* Madison, Wis.: University of Wisconsin Press, 1994.

Hanson, Sandra L. *Lost Talent: Women in Sciences.* Philadelphia, Pa.: Temple University Press, 1996.

Haskins, James. *Outward Dreams: Black Inventors and Their Inventions.* New York: Bantam, 1991.

Hass, Violete, and Carolyn Perrucci, eds. *Women in Scientific and Engineering Professions.* Ann Arbor, Mich.: University of Michigan Press, 1984.

Henrion, Claudia. *Women in Mathematics: The Addition of Difference (Race, Gender, and Science).* Piscataway, N.J.: Rutgers University Press, 1997.

Hynes, Patricia, ed. *Reconstructing Babylon: Essays on Women and Technology.* Bloomington, Ind.: Indiana University Press, 1991.

Johnson, Linda Carlson. *Protector of the Sick (Mother Theresa).* New York: Blackbirch, 1991.

Jones, Constance. *1001 Things Everyone Should Know about Women's History.* New York: Doubleday, 2000.

Karnes, Frances. A., and Suzanne M. Bean. *Girls and Young Women Inventing: Twenty True Stories about Inventors Plus How You Can Be One Yourself.* Minneapolis, Minn.: Free Spirit, 1995.

Kass-Simon, G., Patricia Farnes, and Deborah Nash, eds. *Women of Science: Righting the Record.* Bloomington, Ind.: Indiana University Press, 1993.

Kittredge, Mary, and Charlotte Kent. *Barbara McClintock: American Women of Achievement.* Broomall, Pa.: Chelsea House, 1991.

Krensky, Stephen. *Four against the Odds: The Struggle to Save Our Environment.* New York: Scholastic, 1992.

Matyas, Marsha. L., and Shirley Malcom, eds. *Investing in Human Potential: Science and Engineering at the Crossroads.* Washington, D.C.: American Association for the Advancement of Science, 1991.

McDonald, Ann L. *Feminine Ingenuity: Women and Invention in America.* New York: Ballantine, 1994.

McGrayne, Sharon B. *Nobel Prize Women in Science: Their Lives, Struggles, and Momentus Discoveries.* Washington, D.C.: Joseph Henry, 2001.

McHenry, Robert. *Famous American Women: A Bibliographical Dictionary.* New York: Dover, 1999.

McLoone, Margo. *Women Explorers in Africa: Christina Dodwell, Delia Akeley, Mary Kingsley, Florence Von Sass-Baker, Alexandrine Tinne.* Mankato, Minn.: Capstone, 1997.

———. *Women Explorers in Asia: Susie Carson Rijnhart, Alexandra David-Neel Lucy Atkinson, Freya Stark, Dervla Murphy.* Mankato, Minn.: Capstone, 1997.

———. *Women Explorers in North and South America: Nellie Cashman, Annie Peck, Ynes Mexia, Blair Niles, Violet Cressy Marcks.* Mankato, Minn.: Capstone, 1997.

———. *Women Explorers in Polar Regions: Louise Arner Boyd, Kate Marsden, Ida Pfeiffer, Helen Thayer, Agnes Deans Cameron.* Mankato, Minn.: Capstone, 1997.

Mowat, Farley. *Woman in the Mists: The Story of Dian Fossey and the Mountain Gorillas of Africa.* New York: Warner, 1988.

Ogilvie, Marilyn Bailey. *Women in Science.* Cambridge, Mass.: MIT Press, 1990.

O'Hern, Elizabeth Moot. *Profiles of Pioneer Women Scientists.* Washington, D.C.: Acropolis, 1986.

Pasachoff, Naomi. *Marie Curie: And the Science of Radioactivity.* New York: Oxford University Press, 1997.

Pasternak, Ceel, and Linda Thornburg. *Cool Careers for Girls in Computers.* Atascadero, Calif.: Impact, 1999.

———. *Cool Careers for Girls in Engineering.* Atascadero, Calif.: Impact, 1999.

———. *Cool Careers for Girls in Health.* Atascadero, Calif.: Impact, 1999.

———. *Cool Careers for Girls with Animals.* Atascadero, Calif.: Impact, 1999.

———. *Cool Careers for Girls in Air and Space.* Atascadero, Calif.: Impact, 2001.

———. *Cool Careers for Girls as Environmentalists.* Atascadero, Calif.: Impact, 2001.

Pasztor, Ana, and Judith L. Slater. *Acts of Alignment: Of Women in Math and Science and All of Us Who Search for Balance.* New York: Peter Lang, 2000.

Perl, Teri. *Math Equals: Biographies of Women Mathematicians Plus Related Activities*. Menlo Park, Calif.: Addison-Wesley Longman, 1990.

———. *Women and Numbers: Lives of Women Mathematicians Plus Discovery Activities*. San Carlos, Calif.: Wide World, 1993.

Pratt, Paula Bryant. *Jane Goodall*. San Diego, Calif.: Lucent, 1997.

Rayman, Paula, and Belle Brett. *Pathways for Women in the Sciences*. Wellesley, Mass.; Wellesley Center for Research on Women, 1997.

Rimm, Sylvia. B., Sara Rimm-Kaufman, and Iionna Jane Rimm. *See Jane Win: The Rimm Report on How One Thousand Girls Became Successful Women*. Philadelphia: Running Press, 2001.

Rose, Rose. K., Grinstein, Louise S., and Rafailovich, Miriam H., eds. *Women in Chemistry and Physics: A Bibliographic Sourcebook*. Westport, Conn.: Greenwood, 1993.

Rosser, Sue V. *Female Friendly Science*. Oxford: Pergamon, 1990.

Sabin, Francene. *Elizabeth Blackwell: The First Woman Doctor*. Madison, Wis.: Demco Media, 1990.

Sadker, Myra, and David Sadker. *Failing at Fairness: How America's Schools Cheat Girls*. New York: Elsevier Science, 1994.

Samuels, Linda. *Girls Can Succeed in Science*. Thousand Oaks, Calif.: Corwin, 1998.

Secada, Walter, Elizabeth Fennema, and Lisa Adajian. *New Directions for Equity in Mathematics Education*. New York: Cambridge University Press, 1995.

Shearer, Benjamin, and Barbara Shearer, eds. *Notable Women in the Life Sciences: A Biographical Dictionary*. Westport, Conn.: Greenwood, 1996.

Shiels, Barbara. *Winners: Women and the Nobel Prize*. Minneapolis, Minn.: Dillon, 1985.

Siegel, Patricia Jean, and Kay T. Finley. *Women in the Scientific Search: An American Bio-Bibliography, 1724–1979*. Metuchen, N.J.: Scarecrow, 1984.

Silverthorne, Elizabeth, and Geneva Fulgham. *Women Pioneers in Texas Medicine*. College Station, Tex.: Texas A & M University Press, 1997.

Small, Hugh. *Florence Nightingale: Avenging Angel*. New York: St. Martin's, 1999.

Stanley, Autumn. *Mothers and Daughters of Invention: Notes for a Revised History of Technology*. Metuchen, N.J.: Scarecrow, 1995.

Stille, Darlene. *Extraordinary Women Scientists*. Danbury, Conn.: Children's Press, 1995.

———. *Extraordinary Women of Medicine*. Danbury, Conn.: Children's Press, 1997.

Stitt, Beverly A. *Gender Equity in Education: An Annotated Bibliography*. Carbondale, Ill.: Southern Illinois University Press, 1994.

Stolte-Heiskanen, Veronica, ed. *Women in Science: Token Women or Gender Equality?* New York: St. Martin's, 1991.

Tobias, Sheila. *Succeed with Math.* New York: College Entrance Examination Board, 1987.

Tobias, Sheila, and Carl Tomizuka. *Breaking the Science Barrier: How to Explore and Understand the Sciences.* New York: College Entrance Examination Board, 1992.

Vare, Ethlie A., and Greg Ptacek. *Mothers of Invention.* New York: Morrow, 1989.

Veglahn, Nancy. *Women Scientists.* New York: Facts on File, 1991.

Warren, Rebecca, and Mary H. Thompson. *The Scientist Within You: Experiments and Biographies of Distinguished Women in Science.* Eugene, Oreg.: ACI, 1996.

Wasserman, Elga. *The Door in the Dream: Conversations with Eminent Women in Science.* Washington, D.C.: Joseph Henry, 2000.

Wilson, Meg, and Elizabeth Snapp, eds. *Options for Girls: A Door to the Future: An Anthology on Math and Science Education.* Austin, Tex.: Pro Ed, 1992.

Yount, Lisa. *Black Scientists.* New York: Facts on File, 1991.

———. *Contemporary Women Scientists.* New York: Facts on File, 1994.

———. *Twentieth-Century Women Scientists.* New York: Facts on File, 1995.

———. *Women Aviators.* New York: Facts on File, 1995.

———. *Asian-American Scientists.* New York: Facts on File, 1998.

———. *A to Z of Women in Science and Math.* New York: Facts on File, 1999.

WEB

SITES

F ollowing are a listing of Web sites to visit and gain further knowledge and inspiration relating to science, mathematics, and technology. Can you find others to add to the list? Share the Web sites you discover with other interested girls.

MacTutor History of Mathematics Archive
http://www-groups.dcs.st-and.ac.uk/~history/
Contains a biographies index of famous mathematicians.

Women of NASA
http://quest.arc.nasa.gov/women/intro.html
Profiles of women in NASA

Black Women in Mathematics

http://www.math.buffalo.edu/mad/wmad0.html

The first thirty years of Black Women doctorates in Mathematics, with information about the women and other interesting and important historical occurrences.

4000 Years of Women in Science

http://crux.astr.ua.edu/4000WS/4000WS.html

The stories of creative women of the past.

Distinguished Women of Past and Present

http://www.distinguishedwomen.com/

Biographies of women who contributed to our culture in many different ways.

Biographies of Women Mathematicians

http://www.agnesscott.edu/lriddle/women/women.htm

Biographies and photographs of many female mathematicians.

GirlStart

http://www.girlstart.org/

Organization that encourages girls in math, science, and technology and offers games, postcards, career info, and advice.

Voices

http://www.ael.org/nsf/voices/index.htm

Math magazine that presents stories, articles, and curriculum materials for girls in urban and rural areas. Includes links to additional resources.

Expect the Best from a Girl

http://www.academic.org/

Encourages girls to reach their full potential especially in the spheres of science and math.

Tomorrow's Girl

http://www.tomorrows-girl.com/

Publisher dedicated to fostering interest in science in girls. Features educational books for girls, news, and extensive links.

Design Your Future—Math, Science, and Technology for Girls
http://www.autodesk.com/dyf/dyfmain2.html
Provides practical and inspiring opportunities for young women interested in science, math, and technology-related careers.

Contributions of Women to Physics 1898–1998
http://www.physics.ucla.edu/~cwp/
An archive of more than seventy-five citations of twentieth-century women who have made original and important contributions to physics.

Women and Minorities in Science and Engineering
http://www.mills.edu/ACAD_INFO/MCS/SPERTUS/Gender/wom_and_min.html
Lots of information on the special issues of women and minorities in science and engineering.

GirlTech
http://www.girltech.com/
Devoted to encouraging girls in the use of technology. Activities designed to develop girls' interest in computers, electricity, mechanics, and mathematics.

The Backyard Project—For High School Girls Exploring a Career in Computer Science
http://www.backyard.org/
A project of the Garnett Foundation, the Backyard Project seeks to build young women's awareness of careers in the computer industry.

TAP: The Ada Project
http://tap.mills.edu/
Resources for girls interested in computing.

Cybersisters
http://www.cyber-sisters.org/
A collaborative mentoring program bringing together teachers, college mentors, middle school girls, and gender equity leaders.

EGEMS—Electronic Games for Education in Math and Science

http://taz.cs.ubc.ca/egems/home.html

Great site with examples of creative games for girls involving discrete math and computer science concepts.

Expanding Your Horizons

http://www.expandingyourhorizons.org/

Provides information on famous female mathematicians and scientists.

WattWorks

http://www.tomorrows-girl.com/wattworks.htm

A forum for showcasing the successes of science, math, and technology programs for girls.

Museum of Women in Science & Technology

http://www.amazoncity.com/technology/museum/index.html

Learn about the great female scientists, mathematicians, physicists, and others who pioneered in their fields.

Past Notable Women of Mathematics

http://www.cs.yale.edu/homes/tap/past-women-math.html

Find biographies and academic papers on female mathematicians.

The Girl Scientist

http://www.girlscientist.org/

A virtual community of girls who are into science, technology, and math and want to share what they are doing with fellow girls and female scientists around the world.

Rural Girls in Science

http://www.depts.washington.edu/~rural/index.html

Comprehensive program for rural girls in science developed through a partnership with students, teachers, counselors, parents, and community members to create an environment conducive to rural girls' science and math achievement.

Books about Women in Information Technology

http://www.umbc.edu/cwit/cwitbooks.html

A listing of books about women and information technology.

Contributions of 20th Century Women in Physics

http://www.physics.ucla.edu/~cwp/

An archive of data on eighty-six twentieth-century women who have made original and important contributions to physics.

Hypathia Institute

http://www.geocities.com/~pandoracvi/

A Web site for gender equity in physics, astronomy, and science education with biographies of female scientists.

Explore Career Pathways

http://www.harbour.sfu.ca/scwist/explore/index.htm

A Canadian site designed to help girls 8–18 explore careers in science and technology. Created by a student, the site profiles six women.

ORGANIZATIONS

There are many organizations and associations in which to become involved. Many provide valuable resources and support in science, mathematics, and technology endeavors. Consider participating in those of your choice, join local chapters, or start your own club within your school or community.

American Association for the Advancement of Science (AAAS)
1200 New York Avenue
Washington, D.C. 20005
(202) 826-6640
e-mail: webmaster@aaas.org
Web site: http://www.aaas.org

Association for Women in Computing (AWC)
41 Sutter Street, Suite 1006
San Francisco, CA 94104
(415) 905-4663
e-mail: awc@awc-hq.org
Web site: http://www.awc-hq.org

Association for Women in Mathematics (AWM)
4114 Computer & Space Sciences Building
University of Maryland
College Park, MD 20742-2461
(301) 405-7892
e-mail: awm@math.umd.edu
Web site: http://www.awm-math.org/

Association for Women in Science (AWS)
1200 New York Avenue
Washington, D.C. 20005
(202) 326-8940
e-mail: awis@awis.org
Web site: http://www.awis.org

Canadian Association for Girls in Science (CAGIS) National
6519-B Mississauga Road
Mississauga, Ontario, CANADA
L5N 1A6
(905) 567-7190
e-mail: cagis@julian.uwo.ca
Web site: http://publish.uwo.ca/~cagis/

Girls Inc.
120 Wall Street, Third Floor
New York, NY 10005
(212) 509-2000
e-mail: girlsincorporated@girls-inc.org
Web site: http://www.girlsinc.org/

International Network of Women in Technology
4641 Burnet Avenue
Sherman Oaks, CA 91403
(800) 334-9484
e-mail: info@witi.com
Web site: http://www.witi.com

JETS, Inc. (Junior Engineering Technical Society)
1420 King Street, Suite 405
Alexandria, VA 22314-2794
(703) 548-5387
e-mail: jets@nae.edu
Web site: http://www.asee.org/external/jets/

National Science Foundation
4201 Wilson Blvd.
Arlington, VA 22230
(703) 292-5111
e-mail: info@nsf.gov
Web site: http://www.nsf.gov

**Society for the Advancement of Chicanos
and Native Americans in Science (SACNAS)**
University of California
Santa Cruz, CA 95064
(408) 459-4272
e-mail: sacnas@cats.ucsc.edu
Web site: http://vflylab.calstatela.edu/sacnas/www/sacnas.htm

Society of Women Engineers (SWE)
120 Wall Street, Eleventh Floor
New York, NY 10005-3902
(212) 509-9577
e-mail: hq@swe.org
Web site: http://www.swe.org

COMPETITIONS

Competitions provide a great outlet for sharing your work with others, meeting new people, and receiving recognition for all your hard work. Listed below are several competitions that may be of interest. For information on other competitions consult: Karnes, F.A., & Riley, T.L. (1996). *Competitions: Maximizing Your Abilities*. Waco, TX: Prufrock Press.

American Computer Science League (ACSL)
Computer Science Contests
American Computer Science League (ACSL)
Box 40118
Providence, RI 02940
(401) 822-4312
Web site: http://www.acsl.org/acsl/

The American Mathematics Competitions
Director, American Mathematics Competitions
University of Nebraska-Lincoln
Lincoln, NE 68588-0658
(402)472-6566
Fax: (402)472-6087
e-mail: titu@amc.unl.edu
Web site: http://www.unl.edu/amc/

The Craftsman/NSTA Young Inventors Awards Program
National Science Teachers Association
1840 Wilson Boulevard
Arlington VA 22201-3000
(888) 494-4994
e-mail: younginventors@nsta.org
Web site: http://www.nsta.org/programs/craftsman.htm

ExploraVision
Toshiba/NSTA ExploraVision Awards
1840 Wilson Boulevard
Arlington, VA 22201–3000
(800)EXPLOR-9 or (703) 243-7100
e-mail: exploravision@nsta.org
Web site: http://www.toshiba.com/tai/exploravision/

FIRST Robotics Competition
FIRST
200 Bedford Street
Manchester, NH 03101
(800) 871-8326
Fax: (603)666-3907
Web site: http://www.usfirst.org/

Intel International Science and Engineering Fair
Science Service
1719 N Street, NW
Washington, DC 20036
(202)785-2255
Fax: (202)785-1243
e-mail: sciedu@sciserv.org
Web site: http://www.sciserv.org/isef/

International Mathematical Olympiad (IMO)
Dr. Walter Mientka
Executive Director, IMO 2001 USA
University of Nebraska
1740 Vine Street
Lincoln, NE 68588-0681
(888) 449-2001
e-mail: imo2001@amc.unl.edu
Web site: http://imo2001.usa.unl.edu/

International Physics Olympiad
Site and contacts change each year. Visit their Web site for the most recent information.
Web site: http://www.jyu.fi/tdk/kastdk/olympiads/

JETS, Inc.
1420 King Street
Suite 405
Alexandria, VA 22314
(703) 548-5387
Fax: (703) 548-0769
e-mail: JETS@nae.edu
Web site: http://www.jets.org/welcome.htm

Lucent's Technology Challenge
National Science Teachers Association
1840 Wilson Boulevard
Arlington VA 22201-3000
(888) 255-4242
e-mail: lucent@nsta.org
Web site: http://www.nsta.org/programs/lucent/

Mathcounts
Mathcounts Foundation
1420 King Street
Alexandria, VA 22314
(703) 684-2828
Fax: (703) 836-4875
e-mail: mathcounts@nspe.org
Web site: http://www.mathcounts.org/

Math League Contests
Math League Press
PO Box 17
Tenafly, NJ 07670-0017
(201)568-6328
Fax: (201) 816-0125
Web site: http://www.mathleague.com/

National Science Olympiad
5955 Little Pine Lane
Rochester, MI 48306
(248) 651-4013
Fax: (248) 651-7835
e-mail: Soinc@soinc.org
Web site: http://www.macomb.k12.mi.us/ims/cr/science/so/nsoly/
index.htm

USA Computing Olympiad (Informatics)
USACO
Attn: Don Piele
University of Wisconsin-Parkside
900 Wood Road
P.O. Box 2000
Kenosha, WI 53141-2000
(414) 595-2231
Fax: (414) 595-2056
e-mail: piele@cs.uwp.edu
Web site: http://www.uwp.edu/academic/mathematics/usaco/

United States Physics Team
American Association of Physics Teachers
One Physics Ellipse
College Park, MD 20740-3845
(301) 209-3344
e-mail: aapt-prg@aapt.org
Web site: http://www.aapt.org/olympiad/

SPECIAL

PROGRAMS

A variety of special programs exist that provide instructional enrichment and acceleration in your area of interest. A few of such programs follow. Check with your local colleges and universities for additional opportunities or consult the *Educational Opportunity Guide* published by the Duke University Talent Identification Program each year that profiles enrichment programs in all academic areas across the United States.

AllGIRLplanet Computer Camps for Girls
Locations across the United States

Presented by the Garnett Foundation at eight university locations across the United States, this camp improves educational opportunities and positive social interaction for girls ages 13–17. Girls learn about computer technology, programming, Web page development, presentation skills, interviewing techniques, and applying to colleges. Campers also have the opportunity to meet and talk with talented women who work in the computer industry.

ACEplanet.com
ATTN: AllGIRLplanet.com
200 Arizona Ave., Suite 110
Atlanta, GA 30307
(404) 439-4372
e-mail: agp@aceplanet.com
Web site: http://www.allgirlplanet.com/AGP/index.html

Choate Rosemary Hall Math/
Science Institute for Girls-CONNECT
Wallingford, Connecticut

Residential and day academic program for academically talented girls ages 11–14. Focus on mathematics and science project-based group learning.

Director of Admission
333 Christian Street
Wallingford, CT 06492
(203) 697-2365
Fax: 203-697-2519
e-mail: jirzyk@choate.edu
Web site: http://www.choate.edu/summer/dates2002.html

Duke Action Science Camp for Young Women
Duke University
Durham, North Carolina

A unique and exciting summer program for young women in middle school who are interested in science and would enjoy an intensive learning experience filled with discovery. The camp is designed to build upon campers' existing science skills, promote an understanding and appreciation of environmental issues, and develop confidence through activity-centered learning.

203 Bishop's House
Box 90702
Durham, NC 27708
(919) 684-2827
Fax: 919-681-8235
e-mail: dukeyouth@duke.edu
Web site: http://www.learnmore.duke.edu/Youth/act/index.htm

**Michigan Technological University Women
in Engineering Workshops**
Michigan Technological University
Houghton, Michigan

A one-week residential workshop for girls 15–18 who are academically talented in mathematics and/or science to have the opportunity to investigate careers in engineering and science. Practicing female engineers from industry and the government, educators, and university faculty lead informational sessions and discussions. Each session includes a laboratory experience, a team engineering project, and time to interact formally and informally with role models and talented peers.

Youth Programs Coordinator
Youth Programs Office
1400 Townsend Drive
Houghton, MI 49931-1295
(906) 487-2219
Fax: 906-487-3101
e-mail: yp@mtu.edu
Web site: http://www.yth.mtu.edu/syp

Nurturing Nature and Numbers
Maine School of Science and Math
Limestone, Maine

This camp is focused on science, math, and computers for middle-school girls, grades 5–8.

Camp Co-Director
Maine School of Science and Mathematics
95 High St.
Limestone, ME 04750
(800) 325-4484
Fax: 207-325-3340
e-mail: nnn@mssm.org
Web site: http://www.mssm.org/nnn/

Paula Program
St. Mary's College
Notre Dame, Indiana

Designed for young female scholars entering grades 8–11, this residential program consists of three one-week sessions, each week having a different focus. Participants can select a week devoted to Computers, Mathematics, and Science Exploration, or Visual and Performing Arts.

Paula Program
Saint Mary's College
Office of Special Events
Notre Dame, IN 46556
(219) 284-4778
Fax: 219-284-4784
e-mail: Camps@saintmarys.edu
Web site: http://www.saintmarys.edu/~events/Summerprograms/summer-prog.html

REACH (Reinventing Engineering And Creating New Horizons)
Worchester, Massachusetts

A summer residential program for girls in Massachusetts who have completed the sixth grade and who are interested in learning more about careers in engineering and technology.

REACH
Worcester Polytechnic Institute
100 Institute Road
Worcester, MA 01609
(508) 831-6051
Fax: 508-831-5880
e-mail: reach@wpi.edu
Web site: http://www.wpi.edu/~reach/

ScienceScape
Cottey College
Nevada, Missouri

ScienceScape is a program for sixth-and seventh-grade girls interested in learning more about science. For one week in mid-June, students live on the Cottey campus while taking advanced classes in math and science. From kaleidoscopes to microscopes to telescopes, Cottey professors help students nurture their interests in science.

Office of P.E.O. Relations
Cottey College
1000 W. Austin
Nevada, Missouri 64772
(417) 667-8181 ext. 2122
Fax: 417-667-8103
e-mail: peorelations@cottey.edu
Web site: http://www.cottey.edu/summer.htm

ScienceScape

Purdue University
West Lafayette, Indiana

A week-long residential summer science camp just for girls who will be entering seventh, eighth, or ninth grade. ScienceScape provides young women with the opportunity to investigate such topics as mechanics, light and optics, electricity and magnetism, and astronomy through instructor demonstrations. Activities rely heavily on student participation and experimentation.

ScienceScape
Purdue University
Department of Physics
1396 Physics Building
West Lafayette, IN 47907-1396
(765) 494-3144.
Fax: 765-494-0706
Web site: http://www.physics.purdue.edu/ScienceScape/

Science Quest

Seton Hill College
Greensburg, Pennsylvania

A residential summer camp for girls in grades 7–12 interested in math, science, and computers.

Susan Yochum, Ph.D.
Science Quest Director
Seton Hill College
Greensburg, PA 15601
(724) 830-1044
Fax: 724-830-1044
e-mail: vochum@setonhill.edu.
Web site: http://www.maura.setonhill.edu/~msct/camp/index.htm

Spectacles
Wesleyan College
Macon, Georgia

In cooperation with the U.S. Department of Energy and Oak Ridge National Laboratory, Spectacles is a two-week residential camp packed with exciting activities designed to encourage middle-school girls to see science and math in new ways. Spectacles I is designed for rising sixth- and seventh-grade girls and Spectacles II for rising seventh- and eighth-grade girls.

Wesleyan College
Academic Affairs Office
4760 Forsyth Road
Macon Georgia 31210-4462
(912) 757-5228
Fax: 912-757-2430
e-mail: jallen@wesleyancollege.edu
Web site: http://www.wesleyan-college.edu/community/spectacles/index.html

Summer Math
Mount Holyoke College
South Hadley, Massachusetts

Four-week program for high school girls. Investigations in mathematics and computing to develop conceptual understanding, confidence, problem-solving skills. Sports, crafts, and trips included.

Mount Holyoke College
50 College Street
South Hadley, MA 01075-1441
(413) 538-2608
e-mail: summermath@mtholyoke.edu
Web site: http://www.mtholyoke.edu/proj/summermath

Women In Engineering
University of Dayton
Dayton, Ohio

A week-long residential program sponsored by the School of Engineering that introduces high school women who have completed the ninth grade to career opportunities in engineering.

Women in Engineering
300 College Park
Kettering Lab
Dayton, OH 45469-0228
(937) 229-3296
Fax: 513-229-2756
e-mail wie@udayton.edu.
Web site: http://www.engr.udayton.edu/

Women in the Sciences Camp (WITS)
Marietta College
Marietta, Ohio

The WITS Summer Science Camp is a week long math and science program which gives highly motivated students, entering grades 5–8, a week of hands-on learning in math and the sciences.

WITS Director
Marietta College—Education Department
Marietta, OH 45750
(740) 376-4761
e-mail: erbd@mcnet.marietta.edu
Web site: www.marietta.edu/~gend/wits.html

INDEX